Also by John Gray, Ph.D.

This book is dedicated with deepest love and affection to my wife, Bonnie Gray. Her love, vulnerability, wisdom and commitment have supported me to be the best I can be and share with others what we have learned together.

JOHN GRAY, Ph.D.

How To Get What You Want

IN THE

WORKPLACE

A Practical Guide for
Improving Communication
and Getting Results

Vermilion
LONDON

1 2 3 4 5 6 7 8 9 10

First published in the US by HarperCollins 2002
This edition published in the United Kingdom in 2002 by
Vermilion,
an imprint of Ebury Press
Random House UK Ltd.
Random House,
20 Vauxhall Bridge Road,
London SW1V 2SA

Random House Australia (Pty) Limited
20 Alfred Street, Milsons Point, Sydney,
New South Wales 2061, Australia

Random House New Zealand Limited
18 Poland Road, Glenfield,
Auckland 10, New Zealand

Random House (Pty) Limited
Endulini, 5A Jubilee Road, Parktown 2193, South Africa

The Random House Group Limited Reg. No. 954009
www.randomhouse.co.uk
A CIP catalogue record for this book is available from the
British Library

ISBN 0 09 187674 5

Typeset from American disks by MATS, Essex
Printed and bound by Mackays of Chatham plc, Chatham, Kent

Acknowledgments

I thank my wife, Bonnie, for sharing the journey of developing this book with me. As partners in our own business, she has been a tremendous source of insight and inspiration. I thank her for expanding my understanding and ability to honor the female point of view.

I thank our three daughters, Shannon, Juliet, and Lauren, for their continuous love and support. Being a father is not only a source of great fulfillment but has provided a foundation to create continued success in the workplace.

I thank my editors, Diane Reverand and Meaghan Dowling at HarperCollins, for their brilliant feedback and advice. I also thank my publicist, Leslie Cohen; Matthew Guma, for his editorial support; Carrie Kania and Rick Harris of HarperAudio; and the other incredible staff of HarperCollins.

I thank Linda Michaels, my international agent, for getting my books published in more than fifty languages. I thank

Monique Mallory at the New Agency for her hard work in organizing my busy media schedule.

I thank my staff: Rosie Lynch, Michael Najarian, Donna Doiron, and Jeff Owens for their consistent support and hard work marketing my books, tapes, seminars, and speaking engagements.

I thank my many friends and family members for their support and helpful suggestions: Robert Gray, Virginia Gray, Clifford McGuire, Jim Kennedy, Alan Garber, Renee Swisko, Robert and Karen Josephson, Jon Carlson, Pat Love, Ramy El Batrawi, Helen Drake, Ian and Ellen Coren, Martin and Josie Brown, Bob Beaudry, Malcolm Johns, Richard Levy, Chuck Gray, Ronda Coallier, and Eddie Oliver.

I thank the many trainers for How To Get What You Want in the Workplace who have directly assisted me in writing this book: Bart and Merril Berens, Darren and Jackie Stevens, Joyce Dolberg Rowe, Brad Rowe, Greg Galati, Nancy Stokes, Bob Schwarz, Gerald and Joyce Oncken, Debra Burrell, Melodie Tucker, Wendy Allison, MJ Fibus, Linda Grande, Edward Shea, Margaret Johnson, Margie Thomas, Lynne Feingold, Elaine Braff, Janice Hoffman, Phyliss Lane, and Mitzi Gold. Their experience and feedback from teaching Mars-Venus seminars in the workplace has been an invaluable contribution to the completion of this book. I also thank the other Mars-Venus in the Workplace trainers and the many workshop participants from around the world who have shared their stories and encouraged me to write this book.

I thank my parents, Virginia and David Gray, for all their love and support. Though they are no longer here, their love continues to surround and support me. And thanks to Lucile Brixey, who has always been like a second mother.

Contents

Introduction

Twenty years ago, while developing the insights of my book *Men Are from Mars, Women Are from Venus,* I was amazed by how effective these new ideas were in the workplace as well. In just a few months, I went from a half-filled counseling practice to having a long waiting list. All it took was making one simple shift. With female clients I stopped offering solutions right away and instead listened longer and asked more questions. That's all it took. By resisting my instinctive tendency to immediately offer a solution when presented with a problem, I was suddenly getting many new female clients.

I asked many of my new clients how they had heard about me. Each in her own way gave the same message. A friend had told her that I "really cared" and so she wanted to work with me. It was remarkable. By making one simple change in the way I communicated, I was now perceived as someone who "really cared." The irony of this statement is that I had always really cared.

In the past, however, I had demonstrated my caring by offering quick solutions. Although men appreciated my ability to get right to the solution, I discovered that most of my female clients appreciated it more when I took extra time to explore and understand their problems in greater detail. With this new insight into what women appreciated most, I was able to more effectively convey the support I wanted to give. With a growing understanding of how men and women approach solving problems, I could more intelligently choose a style of response that was more supportive.

In my book *Men Are from Mars, Women Are from Venus,* although I focused on personal and romantic relationships, many people reported that the ideas had helped them improve communication in the workplace as well. Both women and men talked about the benefits of understanding the differences in the workplace. In response to the many requests for more information, I have adapted and applied the basic ideas of *Men Are from Mars* to the workplace. Just as our differences show up in personal relationships in a variety of ways, they also show up in business relationships. Although they are often not as obvious in the workplace, they are there and are often misunderstood. In an environment where people closely guard their personal feelings, the ability to anticipate what others may be feeling, thinking, wanting, and needing gives both men and women a tremendous advantage.

> **Although gender differences are often not as obvious**
> **in the workplace, they are there**
> **and are often misunderstood.**

The insights and principals of communication revealed in *How To Get What You Want in the Workplace* are universal. They apply to everyone in the workplace—CEOs, COOs, executives, managers, consultants, workers, assistants, and secretaries.

Despite the complexities of the workplace with its hierarchies, teams, divisions, departments, and various structures, the communication or miscommunication between men and women determines the success of a company. In every facet of the workplace—from administration, marketing and sales to product development and delivery of services—the ability to better understand men and women gives both individuals and companies a much-appreciated competitive advantage.

As you learn the different ways men and woman communicate and approach problem solving in the workplace, you will have an extra edge to earn the respect, support and trust you deserve. By making small but significant changes in the way you present yourself and respond to others, you will experience immediate results.

In baseball, by learning to become a "switch-hitter," you gain an advantage other hitters don't have. They can choose to bat with the left or right hand. If they have a left-handed pitcher they shift to a right-handed stance, or if they have a right-handed pitcher they shift to left-handed stance. By learning to bat both ways they have an advantage over others who are limited to one hand. Likewise, in the workplace, by learning to respect the unspoken rules and values of both men and women, you will develop the ability to switch back and forth according to what is most appropriate.

Increasing success comes with the ability to switch back and forth according to what is most appropriate.

In the workplace we are often so different that it is as if we were from different planets. Men are from Mars and Women are from Venus. With a greater understanding of these differences, rather than collide, our worlds can come together in greater harmony, cooperation and collaboration. Differences do not have to create separation and tension. With a clear and positive understanding of our differences, mutual respect and trust between men and women increases and all levels of the workplace are enriched.

Without a positive understanding of our differences, many possibilities for cooperation and mutual trust and respect are overlooked and go untapped. Too often men do not recognize the value that women bring to the workplace, while women mistrust the support that is possible to receive from men. Through understanding our differences in a more positive light, both men and women at all levels of the workplace can begin to appreciate each other more.

With this important insight, both men and women have the choice to make a few adjustments in their thinking and behavior to be more respectful of others and get the support they are looking for. Without this insight we really do not have a choice. Without an in-depth positive understanding of our possible differences we will continue to do what we have been doing and keep getting the same results. Too often in the workplace, we blame others because we truly have no idea how we contribute to our problems. Without a clear awareness of the ways we unknowingly block cooperation we cannot adjust our behavior and thereby change the results we get.

Creating Success

Successful people have the ability to express different parts of who they are at different times according to what is most appropriate to meet their ends. For example, the difference between a great actor and a mediocre actor is his or her ability to express authentic feelings in their role. They are able to pull forth a part of themselves that fits the role. In a similar way, to succeed in the workplace we are required to pull forth a part of us that fits our changing roles. The increased awareness of gender differences increases your flexibility to adapt your instinctive style of relating to a more appropriate style. Your ability to create success increases when you are able to adjust your style to meet the changing needs of others.

The increased awareness of gender differences increases your flexibility to adapt your instinctive style of relating to a more appropriate style.

In the workplace, every situation and interaction dictates a different way of expressing ourselves. What is appropriate in one setting is not necessarily appropriate in another. It is naïve and counterproductive to imagine we can freely express all of who we are at all times. Certainly in some situations we can relax and "just be ourselves," but at other times we must adjust our behavior in order to be interpreted or evaluated in a positive manner. Prima donnas may say, "This is who I am and I am not changing," but the true professional says, "How can I serve you better?" and then draws upon the part of him, or her, that best fits the role. The truth is, we all have a little Martian and Venusian inside us. With a greater awareness of what is required, we can then draw forth the part of ourselves that is needed. To succeed in the workplace we have to present what is needed and then make sure that our personal needs are met at home or outside the context of work.

Basic Survival Training

While hanging out with male coworkers during a break or in the middle of a conference it may be appropriate for men to make sexual jokes or talk about sports, but with women present it can be and usually is inappropriate. Likewise, it can be just as inappropriate for women to express vulnerable feelings, cry, or discuss detailed anecdotes about their personal lives and relationships when men are present. With more men and women working side by side, we need advanced training to understand what is appropriate behavior. By just being ourselves, both men and women in the workplace can potentially feel offended, frustrated, or excluded by behaviors that are perfectly acceptable on our own planet. Without a basic survival training for living on another planet, the task of determining appropriate behavior for interacting and working with the opposite sex is nearly impossible.

Even with an understanding of Mars and Venus there still is no clear map of what is right or wrong. Their is no "one way" of behaving. Sometimes a man has to be careful about what he says to a woman and sometimes he doesn't. Likewise, in some situations a woman can just be herself, but in others she has to adjust her natural style.

Appropriate action takes intuition, tact, flexibility, and wisdom. Fortunately, with a greater awareness of how men and women are different, we can develop these skills for choosing appropriate behaviors and responses. With a more expanded awareness that includes an equal respect for both men and women, when we make a mistake, instead of having to defend our approach, we can more quickly learn from our mistake and adjust our behavior. Likewise, when others make mistakes we can be more tolerant and compassionate because we understand the difficulty in determining the appropriate behavior while visiting another planet.

In describing the different men at her office, Sheryl, a popular radio DJ, distinguished Jack as an "awesome manager." She said, "I can talk to him just like I would talk to a woman." In this case, talking about her feelings, boyfriends and personal anecdotes was totally appropriate. Jack had learned to listen in a respectful way. By adjusting his behavior and responses to respect Sheryl, he had earned her loyalty, cooperation and support.

In describing the women in his office, Tom, a sales rep, distinguished his manager Karen as "great." She was like one of the guys, because he could talk about anything. He could make sexual jokes and she would not be offended. He could talk about sports and she didn't feel excluded. Instead of becoming more distant like other women he knew, she would chime in with interest and a sense of humor.

Karen's ability to respond like one of the guys or Jack's ability to listen and communicate like he was from Venus gave them both a particular advantage. Not everyone, however, can completely accommodate the different styles of men and women. Fortunately, this kind of adeptness is not the only skill required to be successful. It is often enough if we can simply recognize, accept, and respect the differences. It is not necessary for men to become like women or women to become like men.

How to Read This Book

For most people, the insights in this book provide a much-needed understanding of how the opposite sex thinks, feels, and reacts differently. In my workshops and seminars, some participants nod their heads and relate to almost everything, while others pick and choose the parts that work for them. I suggest that you approach this book in a similar manner. Consider this book as a buffet meal. There are a lot of ideas to pick and choose from. Every dish is not for every person. What one person finds to be particularly helpful may not be for another. Just take your pick and leave the rest.

Throughout *How To Get What You Want in the Workplace*, as you discover the many differences between men and women, it doesn't suggest that all men are one way and all women are another. Ultimately each person is unique. But when the differences emerge, we need a positive way of understanding them to avoid frustration, disappointment and worry. By having a clear and positive understanding of our differences, we can make sure to make the right impression and create the results we are looking for.

Rather than taking it personally when someone doesn't respond as you think they should, you will be able to fall back on your new understanding that men and women in the workplace have different values and sensitivities. By not taking things personally and by knowing how to avoid stepping on the toes of others, your days in the workplace will be easier and more fulfilling.

Every person has a natural blend of masculine and feminine characteristics. The purpose of this book is not to change this blend. You are already the perfect blend for you. What this book does is to help you understand how to communicate in a way to most effectively achieve the respect and support you seek to earn and give.

> **Every person has a natural blend
> of masculine and feminine characteristics.**

Even if you were to take one new insight from this book, it could be the beginning of a completely new way of interacting in the workplace. I have heard countless stories of how men and women have created positive changes in their work environments after being exposed to this new information.

A Practical Manual for Success

This book is not a theoretical analysis of psychological difference, but a practical manual for how to succeed in business by improving and increasing cooperation. Without having to work harder, you will find that you experience better results. You may find that your work experience is suddenly enriched. Or you may discover why a particular job is not right for you. Whether you are looking for a better job for you or trying to achieve more at your current job, you are now holding a gold mine of practical insights and tools that will assist you on your journey toward greater success.

The techniques in this book are derived from personal experience of counseling, consulting and teaching communications skills, conflict resolution and stress management for more than thirty years to thousands of individuals and hundreds of companies around the world. In big or small companies, these ideas yield results. By providing a broader awareness of our potential differences and strengths, this approach delivers a set of tools to enhance teamwork, improve communication, and increase cooperation at all levels of an organization: management, employees, coworkers, customers, and clients. By learning to promote respect and build trust between men and women, everyone benefits.

**Teamwork is enhanced with a broader awareness
of our potential differences and strengths.**

This book is an easy read for men. It is filled with useful information and insights to understand women better and thereby become more successful. A man will learn ways to build trust with women managers, employees, coworkers, clients, and customers. Since the female population is now the dominant market with greater purchasing power, these insights will give any man an instant edge to get ahead and to create the changes he wants in the workplace.

When women perceive a man as someone to depend on, someone who cares, someone who understands, and someone they can trust, his power to influence dramatically goes up. Ultimately power in the workplace comes from the perception of power. You may be competent, but unless others perceive your competence you will not get the opportunities to demonstrate your abilities. Understanding how women think, feel, and react differently will give men the insight needed to demonstrate respect for women and thereby earn their support.

> **Unless others perceive your competence, you may not get the opportunities to demonstrate your abilities.**

As women read through this book it will at times seem like a breath of fresh air. Finally, things that seemed unfair will start to make sense. Women may finally be seen and understood. At last women have the tools for getting the support needed to achieve their goals.

A woman's challenge in the workplace is much greater than a man's. She has to break into an already existing hierarchy of control and power. We have all experienced how difficult moving to a new school or joining a new group can be. With the new insights of *How To Get What You Want in the Workplace* this difficult journey becomes easier.

> **A woman's challenge in the workplace is much greater than a man's.**

For greater success, change is a requirement for both men and women. Every interaction in the workplace for both men and women requires adapting our instinctive approaches. If someone is from your planet, you will instinctively respond in a manner that is accepted and respected. If someone is not from your planet, it is essential that you adapt your instinctive reaction to respond appropriately to the situation at hand. It is not necessary for either men or women to jump through hoops, overaccommodate, or change who we are, but we do need to make some adjustments. Understanding how men think, feel, and react differently will give women the insight needed to make small but significant changes in the ways they communicate and thereby gain more support.

**Every interaction in the workplace for men and women
requires adapting their instinctive approaches.**

If you were to work in another country, your success would
be directly linked to your ability to speak the language and respect their customs. You would not even attempt to work in another culture without specific training. With proper education,
making this change would not require that you change yourself
or your own values. In a similar manner, by understanding men,
a woman can make the necessary behavior adjustments to be
successful without having to deny herself.

If you worked in Japan, you would not resent that everyone
there speaks Japanese. With a good interpreter or with a good
grasp of Japanese, you would feel confident that you could get
what you need. In a similar manner, as women understand how
to get the respect they deserve from men, the old walls of resentment melt away. By not alienating herself, a woman will discover
that the men she works with will automatically begin to trust
and include her more.

It is no wonder that many women feel unfairly excluded or
underappreciated. In the past, women didn't understand the different customs or professional codes of behavior expected in a
Martian workplace. Without this insight, women repeatedly behave and communicate in ways that lose respect with men.

The improved, supportive, and friendly communication that
results from understanding our differences goes a long way to
create a new overall sense of acceptance for who we are. Misun-
derstandings and the underlying emotional tension in the workplace between men and women, manager and employee, sales-
person and customer, begin to disappear. As men and women
feel a greater support to be themselves, their ability to effectively
cope with the other inevitable stresses of running a business increases.

Great strides have already been taken to support women's

rights in the workplace, but until men and women really understand each other, the hope of mutual respect and appreciation will
remain a mirage. Legislation and better company policies make a
big difference, but it is not enough. *How To Get What You Want
in the Workplace* gives men and women the tools to relieve this
burden without waiting for someone else to do it. If respect can
be earned, then you do not have to wait for it to be given.

**If respect can be earned,
then you do not have to wait for it to be given.**

The good news is that most men are and always have been
willing to give respect when it is earned. Many women have mistakenly concluded that all men are part of a Martian club that
excludes women. Once women understand the way men think,
they realize that it is not women that men have been excluding
but certain behaviors.

Creating Change in the Workplace

As both men and women learn the secret keys for earning respect
and trust in their different worlds, the doors of success, cooperation, and collaboration keep opening. With an understanding
of how to earn respect, we are no longer dependent on handouts.
Instead, we hold in our hands the ability to earn the respect that
we most certainly deserve.

Successful women often tell stories of how they broke
through the glass ceiling by making men their allies and not their
enemies. It is the same process by which a man climbs the ladder
of success. With this new insight about our differences, women
can make male coworkers, managers, employees, customers, and
clients their allies.

**Women break through the glass ceiling by making men
their allies and not their enemies.**

Until a woman has earned respect, often she will be required
to deal with the unfair prejudgments of some men. After applying the insights of *How To Get What You Want in the Workplace,* she will not only be better prepared to break down the
prejudice, but she will have the support of other men. Like a little snowball that gathers more snow as it rolls down a hill, she
will quickly gather more support because of her actions and reactions.

This change does not mean that everything will be easy and
wonderful. Unfortunately, prejudice exists, and in many situations, a woman will be prejudged until she has the opportunity to
prove herself and earn the respect she deserves. For this reason, it
is still more difficult for a woman to get ahead than a man.

**Prejudice in the workplace makes it more difficult for a
woman to get ahead than a man.**

To create a change in any area of life, we need to change something. Fortunately, we don't have to give up who we are, but we
do have to change the way we communicate who we are. We
don't have to change our inner reactions, but we do have to
change how we respond to others. We don't have to change how
we feel about things, but we do have to change our attitude. We
don't have to sacrifice authentic self-expression, but we do have
to adjust our expression to what is appropriate in different situations. With this new understanding of how men and women are
different, you will gain the wisdom and flexibility to make these
changes.

It is a pleasure for me to share with you *How To Get What
You Want in the Workplace*. I have written this book with the

hope that men and women will benefit from this information, and gradually the workplace will change and become a better place for everyone. As this little light spreads through you, may it not only assist you in getting what you deserve, but light the way for others as well.

John Gray
MILL VALLEY, CALIFORNIA

1

Mars and Venus
in the Workplace

Imagine that Men Are from Mars, Women Are from Venus. A long time ago, we got together, fell in love, and decided to live together on Earth.

At that time, we were really much different than we are today. Men nurtured the family by working outside the home and women nurtured the family by working inside the home. Venusians tended to be more relationship-oriented and Martians were more work-oriented. Together, yet in separate worlds, they formed harmonious partnerships. With this clear division of labor, they handled everything and lived happily ever after.

Gradually, the Venusians tired of just taking care of the family and wanted to work in the outside world and earn money like men. They felt constricted being dependent on their mates and wanted to be independent and autonomous as well. More and more, women at different stages of life were becoming involved in the process of earning a living by making a meaningful contribution in the workplace as well as at home or in their personal relationships.

In a similar manner, some Martians began to change. They started becoming more relationship-oriented. While women were wanting to get involved in developing careers outside the home, men were realizing there was more to life than just work. A quality home life with meaningful relationships was becoming as important and meaningful as success at work. Fathers were becoming more involved in the process of parenting.

Although this was a good and natural change, it triggered enormous confusion, conflict, and frustration in workplace. To make matters worse, Martians and Venusians suffered selective amnesia. They forgot that men and women were supposed to be different and that the differences were good.

**When differences come together in harmony,
something much greater can be created.**

As women began to enter the work world, our planets collided. Men did not respect women at work unless they behaved like men. Many women responded and sought to prove their equality by becoming just like men. To earn respect, to become like Martians, these women had to suppress their Venusian nature. This suppression caused unhappiness and resentment.

Other women in the workplace were not willing to suppress their feminine nature. They were not respected as equals by many Martians and struggled to support themselves. They were unfairly discriminated against and were sometimes viewed as inferior or incompetent to do a "man's job."

It was a no-win situation. Women who succeeded in the workplace were overly stressed by suppressing their female nature. Women who attempted to express their female nature in the workplace were not respected by male managers, coworkers, employees, customers and clients.

It was not just women who suffered. Some men were discriminated against as well. Those men who were becoming more relationship-oriented were losing the respect of Martians who were still more work-oriented.

Fortunately, this story has a happy ending. Some men and women were able to remember that men are from Mars and women are from Venus. They were able to respect the differences. These men and women thrived in the workplace and passed their insights on to others.

Women were finally able to understand how they were sabotaging their success by misunderstanding and misinterpreting men. Likewise, by understanding women better, men were able to not only respect women but broaden their perspective and gain valuable insight into being more productive while also improving the quality of life in the workplace. Women found the key to earning the respect of men without having to suppress their Venusian nature, and men learned to achieve greater success without having to work so hard.

> **With a greater respect for feminine values,**
> **men can learn to work less and achieve more.**

Aware men achieved greater success with less effort by learning to create trust, thereby attracting support from the growing number of women in the workforce and in the consumer market. Men and women who could earn mutual respect and trust prospered more and experienced more personal fulfillment at home as well. They became role models and mentors for others. Once again everyone lived happily ever after.

Making Your Dreams Come True

Though this is just a story, it doesn't have to remain fiction. We all dream of a world in which there is respect, trust, justice, and prosperity. We want it for ourselves, our loved ones, and most importantly we want it for our children.

Every man today wants and deserves to achieve success without having to sacrifice a rich and fulfilling home life. Every woman wants and deserves the freedom to choose meaningful employment and to create financial independence without sacrificing a quality home life.

What husband does not want his wife to be treated fairly or be respected in the workplace? No wife ever wants her husband to come home exhausted and overworked, resenting that he has to sacrifice a personal life to achieve success. Every father wants his daughters to have the same opportunities for success that his sons have. What mother wants her son to burn out and overwork in order to achieve more?

Change is in the air. It is time for both men and women to experience the benefits of increased respect and trust in the workplace.

This sounds idealistic, but it is something we can begin to achieve. No government legislation or administrative policy handed down from above can make men and women respect and trust each other more. Respect and trust in the work world must be and can only be earned.

No government legislation can make men and women respect and trust each other more, it must be earned.

The historic increase in the number of women in the workplace presents an opportunity for making significant change. By gaining the respect of men, women have the power to influence the male-dominated work world to be better and more humane than it has ever been.

The new insights revealed in *How To Get What You Want in the Workplace* provide a basis for accelerating the positive change already in progress. By making a few small but significant changes in the way they communicate with men in the office, women have already begun to earn the respect of men without having to suppress their Venusian relationship-oriented nature.

As men's respect for women increases, the conditions of the workplace will change in ways that support a man's emerging need to be more relationship-oriented and to enjoy his life more. By bringing Mars and Venus together in the workplace, a new balance can be attained that will enrich all aspects of our lives. For both men and women, success in the workplace will support the possibility of a personally fulfilling home life as well.

Understanding Our Different Worlds

Without a positive understanding of how we are different, it is easy to misinterpret and incorrectly assess each other. We can easily slip into negative and judgmental thinking. Men in the workplace often make the mistake of thinking a woman is incompetent or can't do a job, and women often think men are either sexist or need therapy. Pretending that we are from different planets makes it easier to observe and to understand our differences.

**Understanding differences empowers men and women
to earn each other's respect and trust.**

In the work world, unlike the realm of intimate relationships, you must earn the trust and respect required to achieve greater success. At work, you don't have the luxury of spending time with one special person who feels a personal commitment to love and adore you. You have to deal with people who often only want the best deal or the most from you and have no personal interest in you at all. You are hired because you can do the job better than someone else, not because you are likable or nice.

The work world is competitive. To be a success you have to earn it and keep earning it. This differs from the world of intimate relationships, in which our primary motive is to give without always expecting something in return. In the workplace, even though we seek to serve others in a meaningful manner, our primary motive is still to earn a living.

**If you want success you have to earn it
and keep earning it.**

The work world is conditional. Sentiment takes a backseat to efficiency. We may want to help everyone, but we can only give to those that will pay. The workplace is not a charity. There are no free rides. You have to earn your way. The aim of this book is to improve communication and relationship skills in the workplace, not to create a happy loving family environment but to generate greater success. Ultimately, the bottom line of the workplace is to stay in the black and out of the red.

Throughout this book, I discuss how our differences manifest in the workplace and how these are often misunderstood and misinterpreted. Each chapter will expand your awareness and assist you in recognizing how you may have been sabotaging your success in the past. You will learn how to begin getting the respect and trust you deserve by making a few small adjustments in the way you interact. You will discover new secrets for improving communication and achieving your goals. Each new discovery will assist you in making sense of the opposite sex and give you added support for achieving your goals.

Life in the Work World

As men and women in the work world begin to understand each other, the respect and trust required to achieve greater success is generated. Not only does this atmosphere produce greater profits, but it creates the synergy and creativity needed to stay competitive in the marketplace. With less effort more will get done.

Even men who are not interested in achieving a more fulfilling balance between work and home are letting go of their resistance to respecting Venusian values in the workplace. They see that by understanding and respecting women profits rise. With increased cooperation and teamwork, efficiency is increased and employees are more productive. In sales and customer service, when you earn a woman's trust, more women will purchase your products, support, promote, recommend, and employ your services.

Women who are more interested in focusing all their attention on their children and their home often find that when their children leave home they are ready to join the work world to balance out their life. Certainly there is no one right way for everyone, but a balance of work and home is an idea whose time has come.

**By improving communication we get the respect
we deserve and the trust that supports increased success.**

Throughout *How To Get What You Want in the Workplace* you will discover the many ways men and women misunderstand and misinterpret each other. Much of the time when circumstances feel unfair, it is really the result of misunderstanding. Certainly not all injustice or conflict in the workplace comes from misunderstanding the differences between men and women, but a good deal of unnecessary conflict and frustration does. With better communication, we can solve problems that have plagued the workplace.

It is not just better communication that will improve the workplace. Men have always understood each other. Long before women entered the workplace, there was discrimination and injustice between men. Prejudice and exclusion didn't suddenly begin when women arrived en masse. The work world has never been a perfect place, nor will it ever be. Yet today we are on the verge of creating a better workplace than ever before. With the advent of more women in the workplace a new opportunity exists for the world. Women add a different perspective.

Throughout *How To Get What You Want in the Workplace* we will practically and respectfully explore the different ways men and women approach challenges and problem solving. By exploring our differences, the overall result is increased respect, acceptance, trust and consideration. Instead of immediately judging or criticizing our differences, we will not only begin to appreciate them but benefit from them as well.

Different ways of thinking and behaving can complement each other rather than create conflict. Differences between men and women are like apples and oranges, one is not necessarily better than the other. A customer may prefer apples, but that doesn't make apples better for every customer. An apple is not intrinsically better than an orange. By being aware of how men and women prefer and respect different styles, you can identify the appropriate self-expression and behavior to achieve your ends.

Sometimes one approach may be better, sometimes another. Ultimately, a combination, integration, balance, or synthesis of opposing tendencies and characteristics can generate a whole that is much greater. You cannot make an apple an orange, but you can create a delicious fruit salad and enjoy the benefit of bringing differences together.

I hope you use this simple book as a map, helping you to navigate through uncharted territories. May it give you confidence and strength to keep trying when situations seem unfair or just don't seem to make sense. May it give you the wisdom and clarity to realize that when things go wrong, there is always a way to look within yourself to adjust your behavior to achieve the goals you seek without giving up your values. With an open mind and heart you will not only find your way in the work world but serve as a beacon for others to follow.

2

Speaking Different Languages

Nowhere in the workplace do our differences show up more dramatically than in the area of communication. Not only are men and women from different planets, speaking different languages, but they don't realize it; they think they are speaking the same language. Although the words are the same the meaning can be completely different. The same expression can easily have a different connotation or emotional emphasis. Misinterpretation is so common and consistent that eventually we develop limiting perspectives of each other.

**Martian and Venusian languages use the same words
but the meanings are different.**

Both men and women form all kinds of incorrect assumptions, judgments and conclusions about the opposite sex, which then restrict or block our natural willingness to give respect and trust. By his choice of words, feeling, and expression, a woman mistakenly interprets a man as selfish and inconsiderate and thus concludes he is less worthy of her trust. In a similar manner, by her manner of communicating, a man incorrectly interprets a woman as incompetent and inefficient and thus concludes she is less worthy of his respect.

It is not that men or women are inherently or intentionally sexist, instead it is our mutual failure to understand each other's language that causes much of the injustice in the workplace. In the distant past, to cope with this negative stereotyping, we lived and worked in two different worlds. There was a clear line separating women's work and men's work. What is different today is that men and women are working together. While this is a great step of progress, it has also placed a new burden on both men and women. Unless we begin to correctly translate our messages and bridge this planetary communication gap, job dissatisfaction will increase and productivity will decrease.

Men and women working together is a great step of progress, but it is also a new burden to carry.

With a greater awareness and understanding of the different communication styles from Mars and Venus, we can begin to solve this age-old problem and do what no generation in the past has ever done. With this insight, both men and women can work together as a team, benefiting from their different perspectives and abilities rather than actively resisting or passively tolerating each other. With correct interpretation, automatically harmony increases and new life comes into the workplace.

Task-Oriented Versus
Relationship-Oriented Communication

One of the major differences in communication is our emphasis on task versus relationship. On Mars they use communication primarily to solve problems and get a task done, while on Venus they use communication for other purposes as well. For men, communication in the workplace is primarily a way to convey content or information. But for women it is much more. Communication on Venus is a way to solve problems, but it is also used to minimize stress and feel better, create emotional bonds to strengthen relationships, and as a means to stimulate creativity and discover new ideas.

This simple distinction creates a lot of misunderstanding and misinterpretation between the sexes. As women understand this point they begin to realize how they may be unknowingly losing the respect of men. As men understand this point they can begin to understand how they may be losing the trust of women. It is essential for both men and women to understand how they may be perceived by the opposite sex.

When men speak it is generally to make a point in order to solve a problem or to gather information to solve a problem. Many men will tend to quietly mull things over, and then they get right to the point when they speak. As a general rule, men who are perceived as competent by other men will use the least number of words necessary to make a point. After all, on their planet "time is money," and more words take more time. Sometimes, successful men talk a lot, but when they do, it is in a manner that implies each word is important and necessary to explain their proposed solution.

**On Mars they use the least number of words
necessary to make a point.**

If a man makes several points, each point must be essential and in a linear sequence to form a logical conclusion. Extra words or unrelated ideas are considered inefficient and a waste of time. Dwelling too much on the problem or sounding uncertain is avoided at all costs. When men confidently speak to the point, they are assured of earning the respect of other men in the workplace. What men don't know is that when they speak this way in a sales meeting, with a client, coworker, employee, or manager, they will often lose the trust and support of women.

A woman is just as capable of solving problems, but her style of communication can give the impression to a man that she doubts in her abilities. In the process of finding or proposing a solution, a woman tends to be more relationship-oriented than men. Her words will convey not only content but feeling as well. Her personal style may sound uncertain and thus be more inclusive. By not presuming to have all the answers, she automatically "gathers in" the support of others. That is of course if she is on Venus. On Mars, her inclusive style sends out a warning signal.

A man mistakenly concludes that if she sounds uncertain or appears open and interested in what others think, she is not confident in her ability to solve the problem at hand. Her inclination to seek approval is not a measure of her insecurity, but rather a useful attempt to create consensus. Her tendency to gradually build up to her solution rather than get right to the point not only frustrates a man but can motivate him to disregard the validity of her suggestion.

On Venus words are used to express feeling as well as content. Women will express more feeling in their expression to "gather in" or include the listener in their experience. This personal touch increases connection. Before arriving at her point, a woman may wander around to build interest and give substance to her relationship with the listener. On Venus, this style increases personal connection and generates trust. What women don't know is that on Mars, using extra words to make a point causes them to be viewed as less competent than they really are.

On Venus words are used to express feeling as well as content.

A woman does not always take time and words to build rapport with a listener. In circumstances in which she doesn't seek to have a personal connection, she will convey content in a more focused manner. In blunt terms, if she doesn't respect a person she will not bother to build rapport and will instead get right to the point. From this perspective, she assumes that a man does not respect her or that he is not interested in establishing a personal connection with her if he speaks in a focused manner. When men get to the point right away, this behavior does little to build trust and will weaken it over time.

A woman will always be more inclined to do business with a man she can trust to consider her feelings. A male manager can quickly create a mutiny of gossip and tension by disregarding how female employees respond to his directness. While many men thrive working under a more direct manager, women take it personally. To make matters even worse, when a man is too direct, a woman may mistakenly assume he is angry with her or doesn't like her. On her planet, when a woman is angry or simply doesn't like a person, she will not bother to connect. She will purposefully hold back from making a connection. To her, it is not worth the effort. As a result she will speak in a more focused manner, choosing to use fewer words.

When a man is right to the point and doesn't engage in a little "small talk" to establish a friendly connection, a woman may mistakenly conclude that he doesn't like her or is angry with her. She will tend to take it personally and feel excluded, mistrusted, unappreciated and disrespected. In reality, the man could appreciate and like her very much.

Four Reasons to Talk

Men at work generally use language for one reason, while women have four reasons. Understanding this difference can open up a whole new world of communication between men and women. By understanding this distinction, women can understand why men don't seem to listen the way another woman would.

Let's explore the four reasons for communicating on Venus:

1. Talking to make a point: Men and women use words to convey content to make a point. In this manner we are the same. Men use the least number of words to make a point, either to convey information or gather information. This kind of communication is limited to facts, figures, and logic, and every word is used to make a primary point. The big difference between men and women is that men primarily use language to convey content, while women may be using words for other reasons as well.

Men primarily use language to convey content, while women use words for other reasons as well.

2. Talking to give and receive emotional support: Women use language to convey feelings. A woman may not be making a point at all, but simply informing you of her emotional state. This is similar to a "For Your Information Only" memo. She is not expecting anything to be done about it, there is no hidden message, there is no request for change or an accusation of blame. She may have a feeling and express it without the intention of making any work-related point. Expressing and sharing negative feelings is a powerful way Venusians give and receive support.

**When women share feelings it is like a
"For Your Information Only" memo.**

For example, a woman might say, "What a hectic day."

And then another woman would respond, "Yeah, it's been a long day."

This simple empathetic response says a lot. It says:

1. "Yeah, it's been a long day" silently says, "*I care*, I am not ignoring you. You are important to me so I am going to give you my consideration and support. I know it feels good to have someone empathize, so I will take a moment to relate in some way to your feeling."

2. "Yeah, it's been a long day" silently says, "*I understand*, I may not have had the same experience as you, but I have felt similar feelings. I know what it's like to feel the way you do."

3. "Yeah, it's been a long day" silently says, "*I respect you*, you have worked really hard today. You have done everything one possibly could. You have a right to feel stressed."

In this interaction, emotional content was conveyed and nothing more. As a result, both women have affirmed their bond of caring, understanding, and mutual respect. The degree of rapport and trust is increased, and stress is minimized. As a result of this interaction, the day begins to feel less hectic.

The secret of earning trust on Venus is to demonstrate whenever and wherever possible the message that you care, understand, and respect. When a woman gets this message, she is able to feel more trusting and thereby relax. Often, the workplace is a more stressful place for women because they don't feel that they are being considered, respected, or understood.

On Venus caring, understanding, and respect automatically earn trust.

Let's explore what might happen when a man hears a woman say, "What a hectic day."

He might respond, "Oh, it's not so bad," "I've seen worse," "We're not that busy," or "You can handle it."

Rather than interpret her expression as an opportunity to express empathy, he mistakenly thinks his uplifting comment might give her a more positive perspective. This is not what she was looking for and it doesn't make her feel "more positive."

When women talk to share feelings they are often looking for assurance. They are not necessarily looking for agreement or to be taken literally, but to be supported with empathy. A statement that shows you relate in some way to her emotional tone helps. If a woman says, "What a hectic day," here are a few examples of what she is looking for:

> "I know, one problem after another."
> "Thank goodness it's Friday."
> "There is so much to do."
> "There's not even time to take a deep breath."

Giving this kind of emotional support is the opposite way a man would react. Men often minimize a problem to reduce stress, and women build it up and then reduce stress by relating to each other. This Venusian process of reducing stress is similar to tightening a muscle to then relax it.

3. Talking to relieve tension: Many times a woman will want to talk about a problem or a series of problems just to feel better. By finding a friend and venting, she feels validated, and this relieves stress. The increased trust she feels when her feelings are in some small way validated goes a long way to lessen stress.

Talking about problems for a woman also relieves tension,

because the discussion helps her to sort things out. Sharing a series of stressful experiences in no particular order helps her to make sense of her situation. As she talks, she begins to realize that some things are not really as important as she thought.

She may talk about what she has to do in the future. This can be an effective tool for relieving pressure. By reviewing what is required of her, she can be more relaxed and capable of getting things done.

**By talking about what she has to do,
a woman can relieve normal job pressures.**

When a man hears a woman venting, he may misinterpret his colleague's behavior by assuming she is trying to get out of doing more. It may sound to him as if she is saying, "I have too much to do and I can't do it." That may be the feeling she starts out with, but that is not the point or message she is giving.

Men also have insecure feelings. The difference is that men don't advertise it. A man might feel inside, "I don't know if I can do this." Instead of talking about it, he will proceed to think, "Maybe I could do this, or I could do that . . . I know, I will do this." By quietly "mulling it over" he gradually feels better and more confident.

A man internally plans a strategy of action to relieve his stress and feel more confident. A woman finds the same confidence simply by expressing her feelings, and then a clear plan begins to emerge. Most men don't understand this process or relate to it. Talking about problems rather than planning a solution is not a man's first reaction because it makes him feel worse.

4. Talking to discover a point: Everyone has had the experience of knowing a person's name and not being able to recall it. It's right there on the tip of your tongue, but you can't bring it into focus. Eventually it just pops up in your conscious mind. In a similar manner, sometimes women talk in a circular fashion, going around what they want to say. At any moment, what they want to say emerges. This circular expression is foreign to many men and can be misinterpreted. Men generally know where they are going or what they are going to say before they speak, but a woman may just begin talking and gradually discover what she wants to say.

> **Men generally know what they are going to say before they speak, but a woman may just begin talking and gradually discover what she wants to say.**

Actually, most creative people, male or female, work in this way. They just begin, and what they want to create emerges. They really don't necessarily know what is going to come out. Whatever is in there begins to emerge through a variety of expressions.

When a woman is able to express random thoughts and feelings, something very coherent comes into focus. After wandering around for ten minutes in her communication, she may then say with excitement, "This is what I wanted to tell you," and then she makes her point.

In this fourth way of communicating, her thinking is vague and unclear, but as she talks she gains clarity regarding what she wants to say. Men who tend to be more sensitive and creative will also process their ideas this way. The problem with this communication style is that a Martian might think, "If this is what you wanted to tell me, then why did you make me wait ten minutes? Please don't waste my time. Get to the point right away."

Blending the Four Reasons

In formal situations in the workplace, a successful woman will tend to limit her expression to the first of the four reasons. She will primarily focus on sharing content to make a point. In other situations, when she feels more relaxed and informal, she will tend to blend all four forms of expression into one. This can be very confusing for a man and counterproductive for a woman's professional image. Just as a woman is concerned about the appropriate clothes to wear in a meeting, she needs to be concerned regarding the style of communicating she chooses as well.

**In a relaxed setting, a woman will tend to blend
all four forms of expression into one.**

When she is in the process of sharing feelings to feel better and discovering what she wants to say in the process, a man may be impatiently waiting for the point. She may throw in some extra small talk or random stories just to experience increased connection. Though this works on Venus, it doesn't work on Mars. A man will tend to become frustrated or just lose respect. To earn respect in the workplace, a woman needs to be aware of how she might be viewed by others and make appropriate adjustments.

When she wants to explore an idea to discover the point, she could say this: "I'm not sure exactly what I want to say, let me think out loud with you." Sometimes all it takes is simply to state what you are doing.

When she wants to express feelings to feel better, she could say this: "Do you have a few minutes? I just need to vent some random feelings. After doing this, she could say, "Thanks, I feel better." This makes it clear to the man that this interaction wasn't a waste of time.

When she wants to share small talk to connect, she could say something like this: "Let's take a break from work for a while," and then ask a personal question. As the other person opens up, it is appropriate to share more from her side.

There could be many ways to prepare a man for the kind of communication you are going to use. The main point is to make sure your reason for talking is appropriate in the situation, and don't assume that he will automatically understand. If it becomes clear to you that you have chosen an inappropriate way to express yourself, then it is fine to acknowledge it, and you will be "back on the team." All you need to say is something light and humorous, like, "Excuse me, I got a little carried away."

3

Sharing Is from Venus, Grumbling Is from Mars

The way men and women relate to stress in the workplace dramatically affects the way they communicate. Under stress, men tend to *focus* more, and as a result may grumble when they are required to change their focus. Women under stress tend to *expand* more, and as a result may need to share feelings when they begin to feel overwhelmed. Without an understanding of how men cope with stress through grumbling and women cope with stress through sharing, both men and women misinterpret each other.

Without this important insight, not only do we miss opportunities to be supportive, but we begin to lose respect and trust for each other. Often a woman will share feelings to get a little support, and a man will misinterpret her and think she is just complaining. On the other hand, when asked to do something, a man under stress will grumble, and a woman mistakenly concludes that he is resentful or unwilling to do what she has asked. Let's first explore how women cope with stress through sharing and then later explore Martian grumbling.

"Sharing" on Venus Sounds Like "Complaining" on Mars

One of the biggest ways men lose respect for women is when they *seem* to complain about nothing. When women share negative feelings in the workplace, men do not hear "sharing," but whining, blaming, or complaining instead. When a woman is sharing a man thinks she is complaining. Naturally his respect for her diminishes.

When women share negative feelings, a man hears complaining.

There is a big difference between sharing and complaining. If you are upset about something and you want someone else to correct the situation, you might find the person responsible and express your feelings of dissatisfaction, frustration, and disappointment. This is complaining. When a man or woman expresses negative feelings with the intent of correcting the situation, the communication is blaming or complaining.

When men express negative feelings to a person, it is almost always with the intent to affect some kind of change. When it occurs, it is often an instinctive reaction to motivate corrective measures in others. Often it just happens and a man is not even aware that he is doing it or why. It has just become a habit. Using fiery feelings to motivate others to change is a carryover from Martian days when men would paint their faces and dance around the fire before going to battle. By making menacing noises and appearing fierce, his enemy would be more intimidated into submission.

In the workplace, if a man raises his voice, he assumes he will be more effective in motivating another to change. He may even pride himself on lighting a fire under someone. While this practice is still common in the workplace, it is quickly being outdated. Getting "chewed out" by a male coworker or boss doesn't work for men or women. Today people recognize that they don't deserve it and will look elsewhere for a job. In the long run this behavior of using negative emotions to intimidate and manipulate alienates others and generates mistrust.

**Often on Mars, anger and frustration are reactions
to intimidate or threaten others.**

On Mars, softer feelings like hurt, disappointment, worry, or regret are sometimes ways to distance a man from appearing responsible for a situation. Expression of these emotions can be an indirect way of placing the blame on others. For example, when blaming a coworker for a mistake a man might say, "It's disappointing that you didn't finish on time." In this case there is a clear message of blame. Or he could say, "With this delay, I am really worried that we will be late." Again, he is not "sharing" to feel better but is giving an implied message, "Next time be more alert and attentive so this doesn't happen again."

This kind of emotional accusation and manipulation is as outdated as using anger to intimidate. Certainly sometimes it is necessary to complain or blame others in order to create a change, but in the long run, using negative emotions to back up this request will only backfire. Instead, by making a direct request for what you want, you can accomplish the same goal and the person doesn't feel manipulated or intimidated. Inspiring cooperation through direct and respectful communication is a much more effective strategy than using fear, blame or guilt to motivate others.

Since men primarily express negative emotions when they are complaining or blaming, a man commonly misinterprets a woman's motives when she shares her feelings. He concludes that she is either not taking any responsibility for the problem or she is blaming him. Certainly women can also use negative feelings to blame or complain, but much of the time a woman shares negative emotions to increase connection with others or feel better. While men hear it as complaining or blaming, she is really just sharing.

A man thinks she is complaining or blaming when really she may simply be sharing.

Most men cannot discern this difference, because on Mars they don't just "share" feelings. There would be no point to it. They express feelings, but only when they want something done. On Mars, when there is a problem and there is nothing he can do about it, a man will try to just accept it. It is done. It is water under the bridge. "Bite the bullet" or "suck it up" are favorite Martian expressions. A man's instinctive motto is, "If there's nothing you can do about it, then forget it."

On Mars, if there's nothing you can do to solve a problem, then there is not reason to be upset about it or talk about it.

On Venus, such a situation is viewed differently. A woman thinks, "If there is nothing you can do about it, at least we can all talk about it."

By talking about frustrations and disappointments, women are able to release their tension and stress. A woman turns a lemon into lemonade by using the mishap to have a conversation, build rapport, and strengthen her work relationships. On Venus, when something negative happens, it is transformed into a bonding experience.

It is essential for men to learn that when women are "sharing" feelings they are not necessarily blaming or complaining. If women are sharing, they are seeking emotional support through empathy, understanding, respect, and concern. An awareness of this distinction gives men a new competitive edge in the workplace to increase rapport and earn the trust and respect of women.

Most men cannot discern the difference between complaining and sharing, because on Mars they simply don't share feelings.

When men don't understand women (and most don't, because men are from Mars), it is very difficult for a woman to feel understood, respected, or considered. She concludes that she is being purposefully and unfairly excluded. Much of the time, however, she is being evaluated by the same standards by which every man is being evaluated.

By remembering that men are from Mars, a woman, at least, doesn't have to take it personally. A greater understanding of men will help her correctly to interpret a man's cool or judgmental response to "sharing" feelings in the workplace.

Applying This Insight

With this increased insight men can learn to be more patient in listening to women speak. By understanding that her process is different, he can push aside the judgments that come up. By remembering that women are from Venus, he can find a greater patience and earn her trust by being a better listener.

By remembering that women are from Venus, a man can find a greater patience to listen.

On the other hand, women can recognize that men are not adept at these different ways of communicating. In the competitive

workplace, where there is always someone waiting for the opportunity to prove he or she is better than you, it's best not to give
anyone more ammunition. By learning to choose when and with
whom to share feelings, a woman will insure increased respect.

When a woman feels increased stress or pressure but senses
that others will not understand or respect her need to share, it is
wiser for her to contain her feelings. At a later time she can
process them with a friend, or she can accomplish the same benefit by keeping a journal to record what she would have said if she
were on Venus and not in the workplace. Taking some time to
write in a journal can be just as effective as talking to a friend for
reducing stress.

**Taking some time to write in a journal can be just as
effective as talking to a friend for minimizing stress.**

Although talking privately with a good friend at work can relieve tension, it can create a wall of separation between those
who are included and those who are excluded.

To reduce stress, a woman needs to feel safe saying exactly
what she feels, even though in the next moment that feeling
could change. By taking time to explore her negative feelings,
positive feelings automatically begin to emerge. These positive
feelings express what she truly believes, while the negative
feelings are mostly temporary and on their way out. In one
moment, she may feel completely unsupported at work, and
then in the next, she begins to remember the support that is
available to her.

It is important that her negative thoughts and feelings not be
freely shared in the workplace. Taken out of context, they can be
greatly misunderstood. Words have a powerful influence. Long
after you have forgotten an unkind comment made about someone else, the person you "confided" in still remembers. Much
to your detriment, they could easily repeat your unkind words.

Either purposefully or inadvertently they could block your advancement.

Accusations, casually expressed at times of stress, have a way of leaving behind a permanent stain. Gossiping, as a way to discharge stress, can be quite innocent, but in the workplace, it puts a person in jeopardy. When gossiping to vent negative feelings is encouraged, it becomes too easy to complain or find fault with others. A better discipline to apply is to restrict mentioning the faults of others while in the workplace. This focusing on the positive is a habit that needs strengthening in both men and women. You cannot lead a company when your greatest assets are stabbing each other in the back.

> **You cannot lead a company when your greatest assets
> are stabbing each other in the back.**

To effectively manage stress, both men and women need to make sure they are not looking to the workplace for all their emotional support. If they have stress they need to make sure that outside the workplace they create opportunities to decharge that stress. By providing life-enrichment programs, flexible work schedules, and recreational perks and gyms, more and more companies are giving their employees the support to get the emotional support they need outside the workplace. This shift has already been shown to increase productivity and minimize work stress.

"Grumbling" on Mars Sounds Like
Resentment on Venus

One of the biggest ways women lose trust for men is when a man grumbles and *seems* to resent her requests. This grumbling is greatly misunderstood by women. When he grumbles, she mistakenly concludes that he is not willing to be supportive. On her planet, his grumbling sounds like he resents being asked for more or that he thinks she is asking for too much. As a result, she feels she has to walk on eggshells around him. Naturally she feels unsupported and her trust for him diminishes.

When a man resists a woman's request, a woman hears resentment.

On Mars there is a big difference between resistance and real feelings of resentment. When a man grumbles, his resistance has less to do with the request and more to do with what he was already planning to do. Martian grumbling is not a sign that he is resenting her request. It is actually a good sign. Grumbling indicates that a man is *considering* her request. If he wasn't considering her request, then he would instead simply smile and say no. By understanding the way men think and react, a woman can more correctly interpret a man's willingness to be supportive.

When men grumble it is not a sign they don't care or that they are unwilling to respond to a request.

Just as women "share" to cope with stress, men will tend to "grumble" to cope with the stress of making a decision. When a man is required to make a decision that requires a change on his part, in his process of deliberation he will often express his resistance to change with a grumbly or grumpy tone. He may moan, groan, scowl, growl, or mumble. In this tone, he may even voice brief objections. This resistance is temporary. It is like a good sneeze. It comes and then it is gone.

The more focused a man is at the time when a woman (or man) asks for something, the more he will grumble. His grumbles are not necessarily directly related to her request or his willingness to do what she is asking for. They are the symptoms of having to stop what he is doing in order to turn in a new direction. Once he is moving again in a new direction his resistance goes away.

Imagine that he is driving his car south and now you want him to turn around and go north. To do this he needs to slam on the brakes to consider the request. A woman doesn't relate to this because she is generally able to continue driving while she considers the pros and cons of turning around.

"One thing at a time" is his motto on Mars. Men can change but they grumble in the process. Women don't relate to this because they tend to be multitasked in their thinking. Without much resistance a woman can consider doing several things at the same time. The downside of this fluid tendency is that at stressful times, women consider too many things to do and feel overwhelmed. Just as a man copes with the stress of considering a change by grumbling, a woman copes with the stress of considering too many things to do by "sharing feelings."

On Mars, while considering a request, a man may moan, groan, scowl, growl, or mumble. It is temporary.

Just as men misinterpret a woman's tendency to "share feelings" as complaining, women misinterpret a man's grumbling as resentment. When men grumble it has a different meaning than when women grumble. If a woman resists doing something and grumbles, then she will tend to grow in resentment. This explains why women will tend to back off from their request if a man grumbles. On her planet, if you ask for something and a woman grumbles, it is a sign to back off. It means you have already asked for too much, and if you ask for more then she will begin to resent you. With this new awareness of Martian grumbles, women can correctly interpret his grumbles and then respond in a way that is mutually supportive.

How Women Respond to Grumbles

After making a request, if a man grumbles, a woman mistakenly assumes he is unwilling to fulfill her request or he will resent doing what she has asked, and she then reacts in a counterproductive manner. She either backs down, defends her request, describes in greater detail her problem, or becomes demanding. Each of these reactions will just increase his resistance and may actually cause him to resent her, when prior to her reaction he was actually letting go of his resistance and deciding to do what she is asking. Let's look at these four reactions in greater detail.

1. When she backs down: In response to his grumbles, to avoid his resentment, a woman will often take back her request with a comment like, "Oh, don't bother, I'll do it myself."

This just frustrates a man even more. After he has gone through the process of considering her request and has said yes, even if he has a grumbly tone, she should not back down. His grumbles are a way of saying, "I will do this but I was already doing something else. I hope you really appreciate it." By having an open and appreciative attitude, not only will his grumbles disappear, but he will be inclined to help more next time.

Just as a woman shares her feelings of being overwhelmed to get a little emotional understanding and empathy, a man will grumble to let you know he wants a little acknowledgment and appreciation for being a good guy.

Instead of backing down, when a man grumbles, a woman should do the opposite of her instincts and just let him grumble as if everything is fine. Instead of taking back her request, she should simply listen to his grumbles and then be appreciative for his willingness to say yes or do what she has asked. Her appreciation will make the grumbles go away much faster. These are some examples of how she may back down after making a request: He grumbles and then she says:

1. "You really don't have to do this. I will do it."

2. "Maybe this is just asking for too much. You don't have to bother, I will do it."

3. "I didn't realize it would be a big problem for you. I can do it."

4. "It is really not that big a deal, I will do it myself."

5. "I'm sorry for bothering you. I can do it."

2. Defending her request: Sometimes instead of taking back her request she will defend her request. This just makes a man's resistance increase. He may then feel manipulated; instead of letting go of his resistance, it may cause him to feel resentful. In this case, he does not resent the request but how it is being made or backed up.

To avoid increasing his resistance, a woman just needs to simply make her request in the least number of words and not be concerned with defending or justifying her right to ask. She can do this if she recognizes that he is not challenging her right to ask, instead he is considering her request and simply resisting having to make a change. These are some examples of defending a request:

1. "You said you would do this before and I have been waiting three days."

2. "I don't ask for much."

3. "This is part of your job description."

4. "We are really behind and this needs to be done right away."

5. "I have to return ten calls, make a bank deposit, and update the inventory. Could you please do this?"

3. Describes her problem: Sometimes to back up her request, hoping to overcome a man's resistance, a woman will describe her problem in greater detail. While this works on Venus, it has the opposite effect on Mars. What she doesn't know is that the more words she uses, the more he will resist her. Particularly the more she talks about her problem. She thinks she is motivating him, but instead she is frustrating him. Instead of talking about the problem, she can motivate him better by talking about how helpful it will be. By focusing on the result or outcome and how that will affect her in a positive manner, he will be more motivated.

When making a request, if a man grumbles, a woman's best approach is to remain silent and just let him grumble for a while. It is his process of letting go of his resistance. When she uses more words to justify her request by explaining her problem, he literally has more words to resist, and so it takes longer for him to move into a more accepting and supportive response. These are some examples of how she describes her problem in greater detail:

1. "I just can't get around this. I don't know what I am doing to do. . . ."

2. "I have so much to do. I have twenty things to do, there is no way I can get around to this. I need your help. . . ."

3. "I know you are really busy but this has to get done. Our presentation is tomorrow and we don't even know . . ."

4. "If this doesn't get done, we will lose this account. I had promised them that we would have this finished. . . ."

5. "We need to do it this way because the other plan failed. I talked with my supervisor and they want it done differently. They think . . ."

4. Becomes demanding: When a woman thinks a man is unwilling to support her and she feels he "should" be supporting her, she may respond to his grumbles by becoming demanding. This just makes him defensive. Instead of letting go of his resistance he may become stubborn and defiant. These are some examples:

1. "You have to do this."

2. "I don't care if you are busy, I want you to do this."

3. "I can't believe this. You are supposed to . . ."

4. "I want you to make this a priority. It is your job to . . ."

5. "You are not listening. I want you to . . ."

Applying This Insight

With this insight both men and women benefit. Women learn how to respond to a man's grumbles, but men also learn how to correctly respond when a woman grumbles. A man needs to know that when a woman grumbles it is not just a momentary expression of resistance to blow off some steam. On Venus, when women grumble, it is a sign they are overworked and need help.

> **On Venus, when women grumble,**
> **it is a sign they are overworked and need help.**

On her planet, it is bad manners to insist on a man's help by continuing to ask. Instead, it is proper to either take back the request or at least talk more about the problem. By pushing his request, he may motivate her to say yes, but she will resent him later. By realizing that grumbles on Mars are very different from grumbles on Venus, a man can respond more respectfully to a woman's resistance when it shows up.

A man mistakenly concludes that if she says yes, by appreciating her efforts, she will not feel resentful later. This is not true.
Just appreciating a woman for her work is not enough. She needs
to sense that you recognize when she is doing too much, and instead of asking for help, offer to give help.

A man also can benefit from becoming more aware of when he
grumbles. He may not even be aware of how he intimidates
women or why they stay away from him. With this insight he can
compensate by making a deliberate effort to be more friendly and
agreeable. He could also lightly say, "Excuse me, I was really
under pressure."

Avoid Using Emotions to Complain

Women by nature use emotional tones as a way of expressing
their feelings. It is a woman's way of saying, "Look here, I have
a really big problem and I want your attention." To set a limit or
complain about what she doesn't want, a woman seriously
weakens her position by using negative emotions. A legitimate
complaint or whatever she is proposing may be minimized because she is expressing emotions rather than the facts.

A woman's tendency to back up complaints with negative
emotions seriously sabotages her image as a capable person and
directly weakens the validity of her complaint. If a woman wants
to stand out with a reputation of competence, then when she has
a complaint she needs to present it without a big display of emotion. Without this professional image it is hard to earn the respect she deserves. There are certainly times in the workplace
when she can be more relaxed and open with her feelings, but
she needs to realize that if she is really seeking to create a change
and men are part of that change, then by leaving out her emotions she will more readily get what she wants.

When a woman does need to complain, it is important that

she do it in a manner that will be respected by men. Straight-forward expressions of emotion are not respected, but objective statements are. If a woman is upset, it is not the time to express a complaint. If she wants the merit of her situation to be fairly assessed, then she needs to first process her emotions somewhere else and then express her complaint in a more relaxed and objective manner. Some emotion is fine, but only if she is able to stay objective. The merit of her complaint will often be judged by her ability to be objective and state the facts and avoid making personal judgments. These are some examples of how she could communicate what she feels in a more objective manner:

1. She says, **"I couldn't believe anyone would treat me that way."** Being too general weakens your case. Instead, you should be more specific and say, "I told him we didn't have that file and he proceeded to raise his voice and complain to me for twenty minutes. I politely listened, but then asked him to put his complaints in a letter." Objectivity is achieved by focusing on what happened and what you did and not on how you felt. It is not professional to share how you felt in order to pass judgment.

2. She says, **"He had no respect for me or my needs."** Putting down a man may put other men on the defensive. Instead, be specific and don't cast judgment. Say, "I asked him to just listen for a couple of minutes and he just kept on talking."

3. She says, **"I couldn't do what I was supposed to do."** Making excuses only makes a woman look incompetent and weak. Instead, be specific and describe exactly what happened. Let others form their own conclusion. This way you don't alienate the opposite sex. In this case, she could say, "I arrived at eight-thirty and the doors were still locked. I attempted to get in but the doors were locked. As a result I was delayed by

two hours." Be specific and factual. Describe what happened and what the consequence was.

4. She says, **"He is impossible to work with. I can't do it."** By blaming and putting him down in this way a woman just makes herself look more difficult to work with. Instead she needs to be more objective and then ask for what she wants. When a woman talks about a solution, it is important to also offer a solution. She could say, "He came in my office and began asking a lot of questions about everything I do. When I told him I could get back to him, he started telling me I had to do what he says or I would lose my job. I would suggest that he get a clear description of my responsibilities so that he understands he is not my boss."

5. She says, **"I don't think he is capable of doing the job."** Instead of being general, be specific. What aspect of the job is he not capable of doing? Give an example. Say, "I have asked him three times to send me the profit and loss sheet over the last six weeks and I still have received nothing. He said he was too busy right now but would try to get to it. I think he does not have the time or motivation to head up this new project. I do think I could do it. I have done this before and feel certain that I could do a very good job."

6. She says, **"He never listens to what I have to say. I can't get any response from him."** This is an emotionally charged expression that puts men on the defensive, and it paints a picture of her as a helpless victim. Emotionally charged complaining never works, and it makes you look worse than the person you are complaining about. A man might think inside, "Well, if you talked to me the way you are talking now I wouldn't want to listen either." Displaying emotional charge rarely wins the sympathy of men, and if it does your image is still tarnished by a picture of you as being overly

sensitive and thus unable to handle difficult situations. To overcome the tendency of sounding like a powerless victim when complaining, the most important thing to remember is to leave your emotions at home.

Avoid Rhetorical Questions

One of the biggest ways women unknowingly weaken their image of competence is by expressing negative feelings through rhetorical questions. To express the emotional tone of anger and frustration while asking a rhetorical question is insulting and inflammatory on Mars. To another woman it passes by as a harmless expression of feeling, but to a man it is heard as a direct attack and very unprofessional. On Venus, expressing negative feeling is a way of standing up for oneself and being heard, as well as a way of asking for support and building a connection. While it works on Venus, it doesn't work on Mars.

A rhetorical question does not seek an answer but conveys an implied message. On Mars, rhetorical questions convey an implied judgment, but on Venus they are used to convey a feeling or emotional tone.

"How could you forget?" appears harmless on the surface, but when it is rhetorical and backed by a tone of hurt or anger it is lethal. When a woman uses a rhetorical question, the implied message a man hears is "shame on you." On Mars it conveys an attitude of superiority and judgment, with the implication that in some way a man is lying, incompetent, or inefficient. Although a woman does not intend this message, it is what a man will hear.

When a woman uses a rhetorical question, the implied message a man hears is "shame on you."

In most cases, a woman uses rhetorical questions as a way to indicate that she is upset but has not yet passed judgment regarding the behavior that has triggered her upset. Women are not as quick to pass judgment as men. They will generally seek to better understand a situation before they make conclusions.

This natural reticence to pass judgment right away does not stop a woman from readily expressing emotion. Men don't understand this difference because men generally do pass judgment before they express negative emotions. This judgment, however, is not necessarily personal. When a man says something is stupid, he doesn't mean the person who did it is stupid.

When a woman expresses a negative emotion in the tone of her voice while asking a rhetorical question, a man will feel attacked and imagine that she has unfairly passed judgment on him personally. He would actually be much more accepting of what she had to say if she were more direct and objective-sounding, like, "This is stupid" or "This doesn't make sense" or "I don't really like this."

When a female customer, manager, or coworker expresses disappointment or frustration with a rhetorical question, it is important for a man to not feel attacked or defensive and realize that she really isn't judging him. A rhetorical question means she hasn't yet formed an opinion or judgment. A rhetorical question is actually a good sign. It means she is still open to seeing a situation in a more positive light.

Generally speaking, she just needs to talk more and her upset feelings will lessen. Her upset is not permanent like a line carved in stone; instead it is like a line drawn in the sand or water. It will quickly disappear if she has a chance to feel heard. If he reacts and defends his position, then she may react, and gradually her line in the sand becomes like a line carved in stone.

Like a line drawn in water, negative feelings quickly disappear if a woman has a chance to feel heard.

This insight is helpful for men to understand rhetorical questions in a more positive light, but it is unrealistic for women to expect their male managers, coworkers, or customers to always understand. If they do, then she is lucky, but in most cases a woman needs to be careful not to alienate herself or be misunderstood. If she does mistakenly offend, she can easily undo it with a little apology. All she has to do is say something like, "Excuse me, I don't mean to sound like I am upset with you."

If a woman does mistakenly offend with a rhetorical question, she can easily undo it with a little apology.

Let's explore some examples of common rhetorical questions and what men hear. Remember, if these same phrases were used with a friendly tone or they were not rhetorical, then they would be fine. As soon as you add frustration, anger, disappointment, worry, or urgency, they become offensive comments of the worst kind on Mars. To understand this point, imagine you are feeling frustrated, disappointed or worried while expressing the different questions. Each of these questions could however be replaced with a more direct comment that will also express her feeling, but in a manner that most men will respect and appreciate more. Here is a short list:

A rhetorical question:	What a man hears:	How she could be more direct:
How could you do that?	You are incompetent.	I don't like . . .
How were you planning to address this issue?	You need my advice to get this done, you can't do it yourself.	This doesn't work for me. I want . . .

A rhetorical question:	What a man hears:	How she could be more direct:
What were you thinking?	You are stupid.	This doesn't make sense to me. I would think that . . .
Why did you do that?	You are inefficient.	This is a waste of time. We could have . . .
What does this mean?	You are being deceptive and can't be trusted.	I can't make sense of this. It sounds to me like . . .
When will you do that?	You are irresponsible and I can't depend on you.	I am really in a hurry for this to happen.
What are you going to do about this?	This problem is all your fault.	This is really ridiculous. To fix this we need to . . .
What am I supposed to do now?	You created a big problem for me.	There is nothing I can do about this. I will need your help to . . .
Do you know what to do?	You probably can't accomplish this task.	This is a tough one. We need to talk more about it . . .
Are you ready?	You are not prepared.	This is a really big challenge. If you want my assistance I am available . . .

A rhetorical question:	What a man hears:	How she could be more direct:
Will you remember?	You will probably forget as you have done in the past. I am not sure I can depend on you.	This is really important to remember. They are expecting us to . . .
Why does this happen?	There is no good reason for this to happen. You are not doing a good job.	This is not supposed to happen. I thought . . .

This emphasis on women and rhetorical questions does not imply that men don't also use rhetorical questions. Men also get in fights with other men. The difference here is that when a man uses a rhetorical question he is aware of the message that the other man is hearing. On Mars, rhetorical questions are used for fighting. They are derogatory and demeaning. Now at least a woman can know why men feel attacked by her when that is not her intention.

Avoid Cross-Examination

Just as women unknowingly minimize their degree of competence with rhetorical questions, men who mistakenly cross-examine women diminish their sense of caring and consideration. On Mars, a man's focus and clarity may make an impressive impression, but on Venus his focused nonrhetorical questions, when backed by negative emotion, make a woman feel personally attacked. She does not readily understand where he is coming from. If he is really looking for an answer to his questions, then she feels that she is being judged for a crime or she is being accused of doing something wrong.

On Mars they think like our legal system. One is always innocent until proven guilty. Although a man is thinking this way,
a woman may get the opposite message. If a man is upset, then
he has formed a negative judgment. This judgment, however, is
just an opinion. It is not as definite as it sounds to her. The fact
that he is asking questions implies that he is still open to change
his judgment. Although he is asking questions to gather information to make his point, if that information refutes his case
then he will back down. From his side, his opinion is not a declaration of her guilt. It is like a preliminary hearing to determine
if there should be a case.

**If a man is asking questions, it implies that he is still
open to change his mind.**

When a woman uses a rhetorical question, she is not wanting
a response but wants to be heard more. When a man cross-ex-
amines, even if it sounds rhetorical, he really does want answers,
and even though he wants to prove his case and be right, he is
usually open to changing his mind after hearing her answers.
Just because he seems so confident in his opinion doesn't mean
he cannot change it in an instant.

This is confusing for a woman because it doesn't seem as
though he is open to changing his mind. What she doesn't know is
that men make snap judgments but can change just as quickly
with new information. She has no instinctive understanding of this
process. Women instinctively gather more information before
forming an opinion and when they finally do it is much more
fixed. When a man is upset and asks a question, it is a good sign
on Mars. It means he is open and willing to let go of his judgments—like a fierce dog barking who is also wagging his tail.

**When a man is upset and asks questions,
it is a good sign on Mars.**

Another man is not threatened by a man's pointed questions. He eagerly awaits the opportunity to explain himself. He instinctively recognizes another man's openness to hear what he has to say. He sees the tail wagging, but a woman doesn't. She just hears the loud growl or sees the intimidating show of teeth and fangs.

The big difference here is that on Venus they need to talk to feel better, but on Mars they want to solve a problem. If a man gets a good and reasonable answer to his question, then automatically he begins to feel more friendly and centered and the negative emotional charge is released.

When a man asks questions with an upset tone, a woman can now be more assured that his upset will go away when she answers his questions. It is time for her to stop listening and give a good defense. Men want her to defend herself at these times. The very action that would be offensive on Venus is actually respected on Mars. When a man is upset, instead of being a good listener a woman needs to assertively take a friendly stand and explain herself.

By staying calm in her defense, he will automatically become more calm, relaxed, objective, and supportive of her. When men get emotional they often need more reasons to become objective and relaxed again. By responding to his questions with an explanation, he will be more satisfied and supportive.

**By staying calm in her defense,
he will automatically become more calm, relaxed,
objective and supportive of her.**

In the middle of an argument if a man gets emotional, a wise woman takes time to rephrase his question and then provide an answer. If she can do this without taking his question personally, then he will immediately calm down.

A man has no idea how unfriendly and uncaring he sounds

when he is angry or frustrated and asks questions that are not rhetorical. When he wants answers to his emotionally charged questions, a woman feels like she is being cross-examined in a court for a crime. Although he is not implying his snap judgments are conclusive, it is the message she will hear. To avoid giving this message a man needs to contain his feelings more and be sensitive to what she may be hearing. By using the suggestions listed in the third column a man can be more supportive instead of intimidating.

When he is upset and asks:	She takes it personally and hears:	How he can soften his approach:
What are you going to do about this?	You are not considering my needs or being responsible.	Would you help me understand your plan for handling this?
Why haven't you finished this?	I expect you to be better.	Tell me what's going on. How can I help you finish this?
What do you mean when you say . . . ?	You are not making any sense.	Would you try saying that a little differently? I don't think I am getting it yet.
What were you thinking. . . ?	You are a fool.	Please help me to understand your thinking about this.
When are you going to finish?	You are taking too long, as you usually do.	Let's go over your plan for finishing this project. Is there anything I can do to help?

When he is upset and asks:	She takes it personally and hears:	How he can soften his approach:
Why did you do this?	You are incapable of doing the right thing.	Help me to understand your thinking about this.
Why didn't you call?	You should have called and now you are the cause of my problems.	What can I do to help? Tell me what's happening.
What were you planning to do about this?	You are very unprofessional: You were not planning to do anything about this.	Let's talk about your plans to solve this problem. Maybe I can be helpful.

4

Mr. Fix-It and the
Office Improvement Committee

The most frequently expressed complaint women have about men in the workplace is that they don't listen. Either a man completely ignores her when she speaks to him or he listens for a few beats and then proudly puts on his Mr. Fix-It cap, offering her a solution to her problem. This man has no idea how he sabotages his work relationship with her. No matter how many times she complains that he is not listening, he has no idea what she is talking about and nothing changes.

In the office, a man will unknowingly generate walls of resistance by not listening in a manner that makes women feel heard. He thinks he is setting a good example of being efficient, but instead he is having the opposite effect. In sales, he often has no idea how many times he loses business because a woman didn't even bother to complain and went elsewhere.

By offering quick solutions to women, a man mistakenly thinks he is making a good impression.

The most frequently expressed complaint men have about women in the workplace is that they ask too many questions and want to change things. A man becomes frustrated when women want to make something better which seems to be fine. As soon as something works, a man wants to leave it alone. His frustration is that women keep wanting to "improve" things that he believes don't need changing. When a woman is committed to the workplace, her nurturing tendencies come out, and she seeks to improve everything. She forms an Office Improvement Committee. Often what she wants to improve first is her male co-workers, managers, or employees.

Without an understanding of how men are different, women have a tendency to offer unsolicited advice to men regarding how they could do things better. Women consider it an expression of support to ask questions and make suggestions when men behave in ways that a woman thinks could be improved. Just as men make the mistake of interrupting women with solutions, women make the mistake of offering men unsolicited suggestions to improve. Men are seen to be uncaring, while women are seen to be trouble-makers.

Our biggest mistakes:
Men interrupt women with solutions;
women make unsolicited suggestions.

These two problems can finally be solved by first understanding the reasons men offer solutions to fix and women ask questions and give suggestions to improve. Let's go back in time and explore life on Mars and Venus. Although men and women today have changed a lot to become more like each other, many of our differences still remain in varying degrees. A deeper exploration of life on Mars and Venus will help us to understand our differences in a nonjudgmental manner when they show up on Earth.

Life on Mars

Martians value most power, competency, efficiency, action, achievement, and accomplishment. In the workplace, they are always doing things to prove themselves and develop their power and skills. Their sense of self is defined by their ability to achieve results. Their success is defined by the results they create. They experience fulfillment primarily from achieving results and doing an excellent job.

A man's sense of self is defined by the results of his action.

Everything on Mars is a reflection of these values. Even dress is designed to reflect their unique abilities to create results. Police officers, soldiers, businessmen, scientists, drivers, pilots, technicians, doctors, lawyers, and chefs all wear uniforms to identify their competence and power.

They don't leisurely read relationship magazines that focus on romance, psychology, or fashion. They enjoy more action and result-oriented magazines that focus on making money, fast cars, and outdoor activities like hunting and fishing. In their newspapers, they are more interested in the news, weather, and sports and care less about lifestyle and the arts.

Martians are more interested in what helps them achieve results rather than people and feelings. In the work world, the bottom line counts most and not personal attachments. Even today on Earth, while women dream about romance, men dream about powerful cars, faster computers, and the new and latest powerful technology. Men are preoccupied with the "things" that can help them express power by creating results and achieving their goals.

In the work world on Mars, the bottom line counts most and not personal attachments.

Martians pride themselves in doing things all by themselves. Autonomy is a symbol of efficiency, power, and competence. Personal achievement is very important on Mars, because it is a way for him to prove his competence and not only feel good about himself, but also attract more opportunities to achieve more success. On Mars, they are always marketing and advertising their abilities. How they are perceived is very important. When women don't advertise their abilities (as a man does) then a man often mistakenly concludes that she has no successes to advertise. Modesty is not a virtue on Mars.

When women don't advertise their abilities, a man often concludes that she has no successes to advertise.

On Mars, ability means very little unless others are aware of it. All success depends on marketing. Understanding this Martian characteristic can help women see why men resist being "improved," corrected, or told what to do. To offer a man unsolicited advice is to presume that he doesn't know what to do or that he can't do it on his own. On his planet, offering unsolicited advice is an insult, particularly in front of others. It says to everyone else that he couldn't do something on his own. When giving feedback in the workplace, a woman will get better results when it is done in private so that a man can "save face."

To offer a man unsolicited advice is to presume that he doesn't know what to do or that he can't do it on his own.

Since he is handling his problems on his own, a Martian in the workplace rarely talks about his problems unless he needs expert advice. He reasons: "Why involve someone else when I can do it by myself?" Asking for help when you can do it yourself is perceived as a sign of weakness.

If he does need help, then it is a sign of wisdom to get it. In this case, he will find someone he respects and then talk about his problem. Talking about a problem on Mars is a clear sign that you can't find a solution on your own. It is an invitation for advice. This is why men immediately assume a woman is wanting or needing his advice when she talks about a problem. This also explains why a male manager will mistakenly judge a woman talking about a problem with an obvious solution as less competent.

**Talking about a problem on Mars
is an invitation for advice.**

When a woman talks about a problem, a man mistakenly assumes she is looking for a solution, when she is just increasing his awareness of a situation so that he will understand the solution she is about to propose. If she is looking to him for a solution, he still needs to wait for her to finish talking, so that she can trust he really understands the issue as she does.

When a woman wants to suggest a change to improve a situation, she will begin by exploring different aspects of the problem. Most of the time, she already knows what she wants to happen but seeks to validate the request by first exploring the problem.

**Talking about a problem on Venus
is not an invitation for advice.**

A man does not know that a woman wants him first to listen and then ask her what she thinks should happen. Most male managers, employees and coworkers mistakenly conclude that when a woman talks about a problem, it is a sign that she is unable to figure out a solution on her own.

A man does not know that talking about problems on Venus is not necessarily a sign that she needs him to figure out a solution. A female coworker, manager, employee, customer, or client is not looking for a man to tell her what to do. Instead, she is primarily looking to be fully heard and then to receive his assistance in making her own decisions. After talking about the problem, she may then want to ask him particular questions, or she may want him to ask her particular questions to assist her in making a decision. To succeed in building trust and rapport with women, a man's greatest tool is to listen longer, ask more questions, and then, if required, give suggestions and solutions.

Life on Venus

Venusians in the workplace respect efficiency and achievement, but more important are values like support, trust, and communication. They are more interested in quality of work relationships and environments than on Mars. They devote more time and attention to supporting, helping, and validating one another. Their sense of self in the workplace is defined primarily by the quality of their work relationships and not how much money they make. They experience fulfillment by sharing, collaborating, and cooperating in the process of achieving greater success.

A woman's sense of self in the workplace is defined primarily by the quality of her work relationships.

Everything on Venus reflects these values. Venusians are primarily interested in working together with a sense of harmony, community and mutual support. They place less emphasis on personal achievement and more on personal relationships. Improving the quality of life at work is more important than producing results in the most efficient and cost-effective way. In most ways, their world is the opposite of Mars.

Venusians don't wear uniforms like the Martians to reveal their competence. On the contrary, they enjoy wearing a different outfit every day, according to how they are feeling. Personal expression and beauty are very important. One example of increasing Venusian values in the workplace today is that women's navy-blue suits are out. A woman doesn't have to do the "dress for success" thing anymore. There is much more flexibility regarding dress, and even men are dressing down.

Besides valuing personal expression, Venusians value mutual support. A Martian will carry one little black wallet, but a Venusian will often have a big wallet or purse to make sure she has everything she and everyone else might need. She will generally have several purses to fit the occasion as well as to match her different outfits.

On Venus, communication is of primary importance. Making sure everyone has an opportunity to voice needs and to feel heard is more important than rushing to find a solution to problems. The bottom line on Venus is achieved as a result of positive work relationships and not the other way around. Talking about successes as well as problems is a way to increase a sense of mutual support, rapport, and trust.

On Venus, morale in the workplace is more about the quality of communication and less about the bottom line.

This is often hard for a man to understand. A male manager often thinks that a woman employee should feel supported simply because she has a good salary or the opportunity to earn more. He doesn't realize that more important than money is the quality of support she receives from the workplace. A man in sales doesn't realize that, particularly with women, it is not the savings alone that interests a customer or client but the quality of personal interaction and communication they receive. By demonstrating that you personally care, and not necessarily by offering the lowest prices, you insure loyalty and support.

This is hard for a man to comprehend. He can come close to understanding a woman's experience of cooperation, collaboration, and support by comparing it to the satisfaction he feels when he wins a race, overcomes a challenge, or solves a puzzle, mystery, or problem. Instead of being goal-oriented in the workplace women are relationship-oriented. On Venus they are more concerned with expressing virtues like goodness, consideration, and relatedness. Venusians will go to lunch to discuss personal issues along with work issues. They are personally interested in each other and demonstrate this by asking informed questions.

On Venus they are more concerned with expressing virtues like goodness, consideration, and relatedness.

When two Martians go to lunch to discuss a project or business goal they will often get right to the point and skip the "small talk." On Mars, demonstrating efficiency and competence is the instinctive priority, while on Venus demonstrating consideration and relatedness are the instinctive keys for success.

More and more men are recognizing the value of small talk to strengthen work relationships. Sometimes a round of golf with small talk is the best way to seal a deal as well as strengthen loyalty. This small talk is expressed on the golf course to make sure that a clear line separates work relationships and personal relationships. Small talk is personal, open-ended, and casual, while work talk is impersonal, more direct and to the point.

On Mars, sometimes a round of golf and small talk is the best way to seal a deal as well as strengthen loyalty.

On Venus everyone studies psychology and at least has a master's degree in counseling. They are very involved in personal growth, spirituality, and everything that can nurture life, healing and growth. On Venus, greeting a person by their name, sending a holiday or birthday card, demonstrates personal caring and strengthens trust in work relationships.

On Venus everyone studies psychology and at least has a master's degree in counseling.

Venusians are very intuitive. They have little antennae that come out to read minds and hearts, particularly when they care about others. They pride themselves on being able to anticipate the needs of others. A sign of caring and consideration is to offer help and assistance to another without being asked. When a man does not offer to help, a woman will conclude that he is selfish or inconsiderate.

On Venus, a sign of caring and consideration is to offer help and assistance to another without being asked.

Since proving one's competence in the workplace is not as important to a Venusian, offering help is not offensive and needing help is not a sign of weakness. This explains why women will freely offer their assistance and advice to a man without any awareness of how offensive and annoying it may be to him. She has no idea that on Mars she could get put in jail for offering unsolicited advice. She does not realize she is giving the message that she doesn't trust a man's ability to do it himself.

A woman has no conception of this male resistance to unasked-for assistance, because it is another feather in her cap if someone offers to help her. In her view, when a coworker offers her assistance, she has a quality work relationship. A woman will feel supported by the interaction. Even if she doesn't need the help, she appreciates the supportive intention. A man may have the opposite reaction.

On Mars, offering unsolicited help can be a source of annoyance and irritation.

Venusians firmly believe that when something is working it can always work better. Their basic nature is to improve things. The more they care, the more motivated they are to point out improvements and suggest how to do it.

On Mars, if something is working, the motto is don't change it. Their basic instinct is to leave it alone if it is working. "Don't fix it unless it is broken" is a common expression on Mars. On Venus, even when something is working, they think, "Let's see how we can make it better."

Any attempt to change the status quo is perceived to be an acknowledgment that it is not working. Any attempt to change or help a man is an indication that *he* is broken. Although that is not a Venusian's motivation, it is what he will hear. Although she is demonstrating caring and consideration, a man interprets it as meddling, criticism, and trouble-making.

In Defense of Mr. Fix-It and the Office Improvement Committee

In pointing out these two major distinctions I do not mean that everything is wrong with Mr. Fix-It or the Office Improvement Committee. These are very positive Martian and Venusian attributes and essential for creating success in the workplace. Long before the Venusians joined the workforce outside the home, the most successful Martians where able in some way to embody both these tendencies. To achieve the greatest success in the workplace both "fixing" and "improving" need to be expressed.

The frustration men and women experience while expressing these attributes derives from timing and approach. Ultimately, there is nothing wrong with creating innovation by improving what has worked in the past. Change is essential for success to be achieved and sustained. With this new insight regarding life on Mars and Venus, it only takes common sense to find practical solutions when our planets collide in the workplace.

Change through innovation is essential for success to be achieved and sustained.

By understanding women better a man can realize when to give solutions and when to hold back. As women understand when and how to express their support and assistance, men are much more agreeable and friendly. By taking into consideration our different needs in a more respectful and considerate manner, men and women can communicate in mutually supportive ways. Making this transition takes practice. By first exploring how we inadvertently step on each other's toes, we can learn to dance together in harmony.

Giving Up Unsolicited Problem Solving

By remembering women are from Venus, a man can correctly interpret a woman's need to be heard without being interrupted by his solutions. When someone on Venus talks about a problem, it means that it is time to hold back from offering any solutions. A man should never presume that a woman in the workplace doesn't already have a solution just because she is talking about a problem. She is often only discussing the problem to get his support for her solution. To presume a woman always needs a solution is demeaning. To be supportive and win her respect and admiration, he needs to instead listen and ask questions.

To presume a woman always needs a solution is demeaning.

Offering a solution when a woman does not want one tends to invalidate or minimize her contribution. Such behavior reaffirms the feeling that she is not being heard or valued. Although a man thinks he is hearing her, he is misinterpreting the message she is really giving.

Here are some brief examples of ways a man might mistakenly give the message that he doesn't want to listen or that what she has to say is not important or significant. Though these phrases are fine on Mars, they can sometimes be insulting on Venus. Whenever possible, a man should try to avoid these phrases on Venus, and instead try saying something more supportive.

In each of the following examples, imagine that a woman is venting her frustration with the printer in the office. Mistakenly assuming that she is looking for a solution, the man responds in a manner that works on Mars but not on Venus. In the second column, suggestions are given for what might work on Venus.

Giving Solutions Versus Giving Support

When she says, "This copier keeps breaking down. I never know when it is going to work," he says . . .

Works on Mars	Works on Venus
Don't worry about it. I'll show you how to fix it.	What do you think we should do?
It's not a big deal. There's another copier on the second floor.	Really, how often has it happened?

Works on Mars	Works on Venus
Just tell Darrel, he'll fix it.	Wasn't Darrel just here trying to fix that copier?
So what's the point?	How frustrating.
I don't have time right now to do anything about it.	Hmm, when did this start?
Well, there is nothing I can do about it.	I know. It did the same thing to me the other day.
OK, I'll get to it later.	Well, if you need my help, let me know.
So, what else is new?	Yeah, nothing seems to be working this week. My phone is giving me problems.
Leave your papers on my desk, I'll get them copied later.	Would you like my help?

In each of these examples, rather than a quick solution, what works on Venus is to offer assistance, give a little empathy, or ask a question. This way he is not sending the message she is a "helpless woman" who needs him to figure out what to do. By asking questions and listening more, a man is able to earn the trust and support of women at all levels of the workplace.

Give Up Giving Unsolicited Advice

Just as men give solutions when a woman is not looking for one, women often give unsolicited advice on how he can improve himself or a situation. When men resist a woman's unsolicited advice, it is because he doesn't want her help. He wants to do it himself. Unless he is giving the message that he would appreciate some help, a man is best supported by letting him do something all by himself. Without this insight into the nature of men, it's very easy for a woman in the workplace to alienate or even offend the men with whom she works. The following story illustrates this dynamic:

Unless he is asking for help, a man is best supported by letting him do something all by himself.

Teresa noticed that a male coworker, Jackson, was tense. He was under the gun and behind schedule to finish a task. To show her interest, empathy, and consideration she paid him a visit and offered a little Venusian support. Although her intent was good, she ended up creating resistance and annoyance.

Jackson was buried in stacks of papers, and Teresa was hovering outside his cubical. Clearly, he did not want to be disturbed and indirectly let her know by expressing a grumble of frustration. She mistook his grumble to be a plea for support.

She attempted to offer her support by saying, "You work in such a mess. I don't know how you get anything done. I bet if you got rid of all this junk and cleaned things up, you could think more clearly."

This kind of talk would be supportive on Venus, but is annoying to a Martian in the workplace. From her side she was saying, "I trust you can get things done. It is just hard when you are surrounded by a mess. I can relate to your frustration. Here's some helpful advice to make it easier."

He responded by being annoyed and a bit offended. What he heard was, "I don't trust you to finish on time. I know better than you how to get things done. You are incompetent. Follow my suggestion, and you will be more successful."

Without knowing about life on Mars, Teresa could not appreciate how important it was for Jackson to accomplish his goal on his own without help. Her advice was taken as an insult because he wasn't asking for help. Martians never offer advice unless asked. A way of honoring another Martian is always to assume he can solve his problem, unless he is directly asking for help.

After learning that Men are from Mars, Teresa was relieved to understand why she felt so alienated in the office. In her attempts to fit in, she was annoying the men. By learning to restrain herself from giving advice, she gradually regained their acceptance and respect.

On Mars, to tell someone what they already know or what they should do when they are not feeling the need for help is insulting. When a man works in a hierarchy, to a certain extent there is always a tension between him and his boss. Men just don't like being told what to do. A boss can ease this tension by giving lots of acknowledgment and trying to give suggestions only when they really appear to be needed. A more enlightened male boss would instinctively do this.

Two Kinds of Men / One Kind of Behavior

There are two kinds of men in the workplace. One will grumble, pout, or become stubborn when a woman tries to change him, the other will pleasantly agree to change but will later forget and revert back to the old behavior. A man resists either actively or passively. He will either consciously or unconsciously repeat the unacceptable behavior.

When men feel attacked or criticized they have a tendency to dig in. A man defends himself by not changing. He continues to do the same behavior seeking to prove its validity. A woman may consider this petty, and it is, but women also become defensive. They just do it in a different way. A woman will tend to justify a mood when a man tries to minimize it. If a man says a woman is getting upset over nothing or making a big deal out of nothing, she will tend to persist in being upset to justify the validity of her feelings.

If a woman is to create rapport and connection with a man, she can best do this by giving up trying to improve him. The following chart summarizes the ways a woman can give up trying to improve a man:

How to Give Up Trying to Improve a Man

What she needs to remember:	What she can do or not do:
Don't ask him too many questions when he is annoyed, or he will feel you are trying to change him.	Ignore that he is annoyed unless he wants to talk to you about it. If you say, "What's up?" and he says, "Nothing," then let it go.
Give up trying to comfort him in any way. His grumbles about something are not an invitation for advice.	Make sure you don't take sides with someone who bothers him. A woman will attempt to calm a man by pointing out why the person with whom he is upset is really not so bad.
When you offer unsolicited advice, he may become offended and feel as if he is being perceived as incapable of handling a situation.	Practice patience and trust that he can handle it on his own. If he needs help, he will ask for it. If you don't feel a need to give help, he will feel more inclined to ask for help.
When a man resists a request, he is just temporarily grumbling. It doesn't mean he will resent you for making the request.	After making a request, don't say anything. Let him grumble without trying to explain why he should want to do something. Once he does it, forget that he grumbled and be appreciative that he did what you asked.

What she needs to remember:	What she can do or not do:
If you make sacrifices hoping a man will change, he will feel pressured to change and resist you more.	Don't make sacrifices to justify a request. Instead, just ask directly for what you want. If he says no, ask again and be willing to negotiate. Men appreciate directness.
If you can be accepting of his differences, he will be more understanding of you.	Relax and surrender your tendency to make him better. Practice accepting imperfection. Make his feelings more important than perfection and don't lecture or correct him.
Men need to save face in front of others.	Be careful not to correct him in front of others. Score big points by minimizing his mistakes with comments like, "It's no problem" or "It's not a big deal."

In any situation in the workplace, if you give unsolicited advice to a man, you will be received with less resistance by helping him to save face and not appear incompetent. Sometimes a woman's job description requires that she give advice to a man. Here are six tips for minimizing tension when you have to give a man unsolicited advice.

Six Tips for Giving Unsolicited Advice

1. Direct requests are generally more readily received than suggestions and advice. Instead of saying, "You should clean the filters when you are done," you can say, "Would you clean

the filters when you are done?" or "Please clean the filters when you are done."

2. When making a request use "would you" instead of "could you." "Could you" is indirect, while "Would you" is direct and implies a trust that he can do what you are asking. Instead of saying, "*Could* you look this over again?" make your request direct by saying, "*Would* you look this over?"

3. State the simple facts and use the least amount of words. For example, "The paint is still wet." He doesn't need someone to tell him to be careful or to keep his hands off the wall.

4. Don't presume to know something he doesn't. This suggests you think you know more than he. You can give your experience. Instead of saying, "Don't worry, planes are always late," you could say, "I wouldn't worry. Planes are always late when I travel."

5. Don't presume that he needs help. Instead of saying, "The paper is in the bottom drawer," you could say, "In case you didn't know, the paper is in the bottom drawer."

6. Don't presume that he is asking for your opinion. Say what you think, in a casual way: "I think . . . we are not obligated in any way to finish this report."

These six tips are particularly helpful for male and female managers directing male employees because their responsibilities require giving direction and advice. These approaches will be helpful for a woman at any level of the workplace for giving advice when it is her business and seems necessary.

These are some lead-in comments that make unsolicited advice and suggestions less demeaning on Mars:

1. "I have a suggestion that might be helpful . . ."

2. "If you want to know what I think . . ."

3. "You probably already know this, but . . ."

4. "You probably have already considered this, but just in case . . ."

5. "I know you didn't ask for help, but just in case . . ."

6. "Would you try . . ."

7. "If you want any help on this give me a call . . ."

8. "As a favor, would you . . ."

9. "The mail room closes in ten minutes, would you . . ."

10. "If you asked me, I would say . . ."

As an exercise in understanding how men react, women readers can try thinking of situations where they might apply the above "face-saving" lead-in phrases. Men readers can reflect on times when they felt annoyed by a woman's unsolicited advice and consider that she was only trying to be helpful and didn't imply mistrust in his abilities.

Applying the Tips for Giving Unsolicited Advice

These phrases will not always work, but they will help. Sometimes unsolicited advice will annoy a man no matter what. Showing extra consideration through using the six tips will cause him to grumble less and forget it quickly.

Let's now apply this insight for giving advice and direction. Keep in mind that when a man is clearly asking for help, these tips are not required. On Mars, direct advice is only insulting when it is unsolicited. Here are ten examples of giving unsolicited advice with corresponding examples of ways to avoid insulting him by saving face.

Giving Unsolicited Advice

Are you going to call the sales department? I'm sure they will want to know the status of this order. Could you give them a call?

Make sure you tell Harry we still haven't received his letter.

You are not allowed to use this copier. You could get in trouble.

Where are you going? You still need to meet with the buyers. If you go now, you may not get back in time.

Take a little time to collect yourself and review your notes before you come in to make your presentation.

You shouldn't be taking so much time on the expansion project. We still have to finish the Christmas orders.

You don't need to pay so much. I know where you can buy these for half the price.

Saving Face

I don't know if you heard but the sales department called about the status of this order. They seemed anxious. Would you give them a call?

If you talk to Harry, would you do me a favor and let him know we haven't received his letter?

Just in case you didn't know, Richard counts the paper in this copier.

You probably know this, but just in case, the buyers will be here at 4 o'clock.

I'm not in a hurry. It's fine with me if you want to take a little time to review your notes before making the presentation.

I'm feeling pressured by these Christmas orders. Would you schedule some time to help me?

I have a suggestion that might be helpful. You can buy these for about half the price in New Orleans.

Giving Unsolicited Advice	Saving Face
You don't need a new laptop. All you need is a bigger hard drive. The old one can be replaced without having to buy a whole new computer.	You probably already know this, but if you only want a bigger hard drive for your laptop, you can replace it without getting a new computer.
You are not giving yourself enough time. You should at least call and let them know you might be late.	It's already 3:30. Would you give them a call.
I think if you listen to what she is saying, she might forget the whole thing and drop the case.	If I were her, I would probably forget the whole case if I thought you really understood. She probably needs to vent her feelings to feel heard.

For a woman to win the respect and support of men in the workplace, learning when and how to give advice is tremendously helpful and greatly appreciated by men. On the other hand, when women give unsolicited advice and a man grumbles or seems irritated, it is easy for women to take his response the wrong way and feel rejected, dismissed, or demeaned. Rather than grumbling and being annoyed with a woman's advice, a man can learn some alternative responses.

It is unrealistic just to say "don't grumble" or "don't be annoyed." If you are annoyed, there is little you can do. Even if you hold it in, she will still feel your rejection. A way to avoid this is to express a response that can be authentic and respectful. Though these responses aren't needed on Mars, they are on Venus. By having a "comeback" supportive statement, a man is more at ease. As a result, his female manager, coworker, employee, client, or customer is put at ease as well. Let's look at some examples. Keep in mind that in different situations each phrase might be more or less appropriate.

Seven "Comeback" Statements for Men

In this situation, imagine a man ready to make a call. He has it on his list of things to do, but is presently focusing on something else he considers more important and is feeling frustrated. His coworker Linda steps in his office and says, "It's already three o'clock. You should call Sam right away."

In that instant, all the frustration he is feeling about the project on which he is working gets focused on her. By making a comeback statement, he can easily diffuse the situation for himself and her. These statements will take the edge off his resistance that has been displaced onto Linda. Instead of glaring or grumbling, he could take a deep breath to calm himself for a moment and then respond with any of the following statements:

1. He can make light of it by taking a deep breath and saying, "Thank you for sharing."

2. He could take a deep breath and say in a confident and reassuring tone, "It will be done" or "I'll do it right away."

3. He could take a deep breath and sincerely say, "I knew that, but thanks for helping."

4. He could take a deep breath and say in a friendly tone, "*You* . . . are right."

5. He could take a deep breath and politely say, "I was planning to call him this afternoon, but since you reminded me I might as well do it now."

6. He could take a deep breath and then say in a humble and easy manner, "OK," "Sure," or "No problem."

7. He could take a deep breath, take a long stretch, and then say in a respectful way, "It would be my pleasure" or "I will be happy to call Sam right away."

By taking a deep breath, he is able to center himself. More important he gives a clear message that he is taking responsibility to communicate in a manner that doesn't blame her for his frustration. The act of taking a deep breath acknowledges that he was already frustrated and that she is not the source of his annoyance. This action allows a man to realize he is responsible for his frustration. As a result, he can more freely release it and communicate in a manner that will build trust and respect.

As men and women both learn to respect their different styles and needs in the workplace, communication improves and tension is reduced. With this insight, being a Mr. Fix-It from Mars or being a member of the Office Improvement Committee from Venus need not be a liability but an asset. It is a pleasure to work with people when you can anticipate getting your needs met as well as meeting theirs. To achieve this goal, men and women need practice in the art of listening to what is really being said and responding in a way that is respectful and considerate.

5

Men Go to Their Caves
and Women Talk

One of the biggest differences between men and women in the workplace is how they approach solving problems. When faced with a problem, a man's first reaction is to go to his cave and solve it on his own, but a woman's first reaction is to reach out and include others through talking about it. As a result, men appear to be more assertive and women appear to be more willing to collaborate. This difference, when not understood, creates friction and tension between the sexes.

Solving Problems on Mars

On Mars, a man will first assess a problem by considering how he can solve it alone. When he can solve a problem on his own, it stimulates confidence and the energy to get things done. If he has to wait for others before he can do something about it, his stress level increases. Having to depend on others, when it is not necessary, is a waste of his time and energy. To minimize this stress, his tendency will be to lead or to follow. Either he wants to do it all or he will get out of the way and support another in doing it. Collaboration is not his comfort zone.

Having to depend on others, when it is not necessary, seems like a waste of his time and energy.

Besides reducing stress, independent action often earns greater acknowledgment. In a basketball game, many players may score points, but at the end, he who scores the point that wins the game is seen as the champion. It is natural to seek credit, and this is particularly true in the workplace. Problems may get solved, but if others don't recognize that you were responsible, then you don't get the credit.

Men define themselves and each other through the yardstick of their actions, results, and achievements. Salary increases, job advancement, increased market share, and increased sales all result from the accumulation of "credit" for your achievements. You can be one of the leading experts in your field, but if no one knows, you don't get the opportunities you deserve.

Solving Problems on Venus

On Venus they regard problems in a different light. The action of solving a problem is an opportunity to demonstrate sharing, cooperation, and collaboration. From a woman's perspective, if one can do the job, then maybe two can do a better job. On her planet, all those capable of offering competent support to solving a problem are included in the process.

Women demonstrate respect and appreciation by being inclu-

sive of others in the process of solving a problem. To exclude another implies that they are not respected as equals or are not
considered competent to offer assistance. When others are not
included in the process of problem solving, it is easy to take it
personally or feel offended.

Even if a woman feels she is capable of solving a problem
alone, she will still respect the needs of others and include them. In
this way, she builds trusting work relationships. By sharing a problem with another, she is in no way implying that she could not
come up with a solution on her own. Her focus of attention, unlike a man, is not wrapped up in proving she can get the job done.
Instead, she wants to give coworkers, managers, or employees the
opportunity to become involved in solving the problem.

> **By sharing a problem, a woman is not implying that she
> could not come up with a solution on her own.**

On Venus, sharing a problem is also a way to most effectively
solve a problem. A variety of benefits may or may not occur. It
could be that a coworker has a similar problem that could be
solved at the same time. It could be that a coworker is already
doing something that could be a solution to the problem, and thus
an independent solution would be redundant. It could be that a
coworker has extra resources to offer in the process of solving the
problem. From this perspective, sharing a problem is like planting
seeds in the garden. You never know which one will sprout, but it
would be foolish not to try. Most importantly, coworkers get the
idea that their needs and talents are not being overlooked.

Solving Problems in His Cave

For many men, their ability to get ahead and achieve greater success is directly related to their ability to block out all distractions

and focus on one task. On Mars, this is called going to his cave. In his cave, he will push away the world with all its distractions and focus on finding solutions. When he is not interacting with others he can quietly think things through or "mull things over." For example, a professional baseball pitcher is able to block out a stadium of screaming fans to prepare calmly for his perfect pitch.

Every Martian has to find a cave that allows him to block out the world and focus his full attention on one task. The more important the task, the deeper into his cave he will go. At such times, he is unaware of others and doesn't like being interrupted or distracted.

Every Martian has a cave that allows him to block out the world and focus his full attention on one task.

By going into his cave, a man can clearly focus his mind on finding a solution. When a problem is presented to a man, he either needs to do something about it or he puts it in the "to be handled later" file. This way he doesn't have to dwell too long on the problem.

Coping with Stress in His Cave

When a problem is being discussed and not solved it is a source of greater stress for a man. Men have less tolerance for emotional distress than women. When presented with a problem, by nature a man feels a greater urgency to find a solution or do something about it. The very act of developing a plan of action to solve a problem helps to minimize his stress. More discussion will just make it worse.

Men have less tolerance for emotional distress than women.

Listening to a woman discuss a problem in more detail than he thinks is required to solve the problem makes him increasingly impatient and frustrated. He wants to move from analyzing the problem to solving it. Through withdrawing into his cave to focus on a solution, he can begin to relax. If he can't find a solution, then to minimize stress he will temporarily forget the problem by focusing on something else that he *can* do something about.

**Action is most relaxing for him, while talking is often
more relaxing for women.**

By doing something challenging on his own, hormones get released that help him to forget other more pressing problems and relax the work-oriented, responsible part of his brain. Plato first pointed out this stress-reduction technique. Stress increases by using one part of the brain all the time. By shifting gears and using another part of the brain, the overworked part can rest. In making this point, Plato was explaining the purpose of recreation and playful sport.

**Plato observed that by shifting gears to use another part
of the brain, the overworked part can rest.**

When men focus on a problem without finding a solution, they become increasingly stressed. By temporarily using another part of the brain, the stressed part can rest and rejuvenate. When the "play" part of the brain is activated, the work part can take a nap. This begins to generate feel-good endorphins and chemicals in his body. By doing something engaging, fun, or entertaining, a man can temporarily forget his stress.

Coping with Stress in a Group

Stress often increases when a group of men and women get together to discuss a problem. As the women continue to explore the problem through sharing and listening they are able to better cope with the stress. The men, however, need to feel as if something is being done or being accomplished by this talk, otherwise they become very impatient and stressed. Men keep interrupting to offer solutions, frustrating women, while women keep exploring the problem, and then they explore their problems with the various suggested solutions. Without an understanding of our differences, men and women in the workplace are at odds.

Stress often increases when a group of men and women get together to discuss a problem.

Wise men need to accept that sometimes the best solution is to let everyone talk. By keeping this awareness of the importance of talk for women, a man can relax and realize that by listening and being patient he is scoring big points with his coworkers. Although by listening he may not be solving the problem at hand, he is solving a much bigger problem, which is making sure the women feel heard. Likewise, wise women can recognize that by getting more to the point they score points with male coworkers.

Getting to the point right away doesn't mean women have to talk less. Women often don't speak out enough. In a group meeting, men will tend to talk a lot more, while a woman will tend to speak less, allowing others a fair share of time to talk. On her planet, she is being polite, but on Mars she is seen as not having much to say.

By talking less, a woman thinks she is being polite, but on Mars she is seen as not having much to say.

When a group of women have a meeting they will have a greater sense of including others in the conversation and being careful to not dominate by talking too much. When meeting with men, a woman needs to be aware that men are following Martian rules and manners. It is fine for her to speak up without being asked, and to take longer expressing her solutions and suggestions.

She may have concluded that the men are not interested in what she has to say, because she could sense their impatience when she speaks. This only occurs if she dwells too long on the problem or doesn't focus on a solution. It is generally taking more time to talk about problems that frustrates the men and not what she has to say about the solution.

The Dragon in the Cave

When men become grumpy or irritable it is often a symptom of being in their caves. When a man wants to get something done, he becomes temporarily irritable and grumbly if he feels obstructed, postponed, or distracted. Women need to understand this symptom, otherwise they take his grumbles personally.

On Mars, every cave has a sign that reads, "Do not disturb or be burned by the dragon." Men naturally give a man lots of space when he is in his cave. They know that he will come out when he has a clear idea of the solution he is looking for. If they see a little dragon smoke, they don't worry, because they know that the dragon never emerges. You can only get burned by the dragon by going into his cave.

> **On Mars, every cave has a sign that reads, "Do not disturb or be burned by the dragon."**

Men instinctively understand this sign, but on Venus the message means something else. It means, "I have a problem and don't know where to turn for help. If you can help, please come in and offer your assistance."

When a woman appears withdrawn or more independent, often she would appreciate someone offering assistance and support. Some women are not very good at asking for support directly, and one way they do it indirectly is by making it clear that they are doing something all by themselves. This independence is an invitation for help.

When a man pulls back into his cave, a woman will misinterpret his need for space as a need for assistance and reassurance. A woman will tend to go into his cave offering her assistance and support by asking a lot of questions. After doing what she thinks is the supportive thing, it is even more confusing for her when he becomes annoyed and grumpy or is short with her or in a hurry. His behavior makes her feel unimportant to him and generates a feeling of distance and mistrust.

> **A woman will misinterpret a man's need for space as a need for assistance and reassurance.**

The tendency to pull back into the cave and become temporarily irritated by intrusions is a function of one's level of testosterone. Most men have much higher levels of testosterone and thus will demonstrate cave behavior to a greater extent. Most women do not have high testosterone levels, and as a result they have difficulty understanding a man's hot and cold reactions.

By understanding a man's cave tendencies, a woman can learn to not take his behavior personally and to respect his need for space. If she needs to talk with him when he is in his cave, this can still be accomplished. She needs to let him know how much time she requires from him to discuss certain issues. Then she should be prepared to let him know exactly what topics she wants to go over. This kind of precision and focus will assist him in shifting his attention to her without any irritation.

**When a man is in his cave, begin a conversation by
letting him know up front how much time is required.**

Understanding the psychology of men and their caves is essential survival training for any woman in the workplace. Whether you are being managed by a man or you are managing men, many problems can be avoided by correctly interpreting his cave time.

Men must realize that most women will misinterpret their cave time. They will take it personally and withdraw their support for a variety of reasons. Even though their reaction is a misinterpretation of his indifferent and impersonal mood, he will still suffer the consequences. A male manager or coworker can stimulate a more positive feeling of mutual respect and cooperation by taking this difference into consideration. By practicing a little restraint in his grumbles, he can prevent a host of work relationship problems down the line.

A male dentist, for example, who demonstrates a friendly warmth and consideration to his assistants (male or female), particularly in the presence of a female patient, will earn her loyalty and support. Women are particularly sensitive to how people are being treated. In every field, success is determined by repeat business and referrals. This is insured when women see that a person is considerate of others.

In many cases, all it takes is softening the sharp edges of cave behavior by purposely adding a few extra friendly words like, "Would you please . . . , That's OK . . . , Thank you . . . , good, nice work, good job," etc.

**When a man is independently performing a work task,
he is often unaware of how
his cave persona affects others.**

A positive attitude about the workplace has a dramatic impact on the success of the business. Men in leadership roles often sabotage their success by not understanding how their cave behavior may be easily misinterpreted. With this insight, he can often correct the situation by demonstrating a little more consideration.

How Women React to the Cave

Cave behavior can be read in very negative ways by women. Here are some perceived characteristics:

1. **Excluding:** A woman may feel excluded and feel as if her abilities are not appreciated, acknowledged, or respected. She will have difficulty connecting and participating in a graceful manner.

2. **Uncaring:** A woman may feel that he doesn't care what she thinks or that her input is not valued by him.

3. **No time:** A woman may think that he doesn't have the time to talk to her or have any interest in what she can offer.

4. **Impersonal:** A woman may believe that all he cares about is the bottom line and that her personal needs are not important to him at all. She will not trust him to look out for her needs in a transaction.

5. **Intimidating:** A woman may feel intimidated, as if nothing she does is good enough for him. This creates fear and a tendency to distance herself.

6. **Misunderstands:** A woman will believe he does not understand her motives. Above all else, if she is to do business with someone or trust them as a coworker or manager, a woman needs to feel that she is understood in a positive light.

7. **Unapproachable:** A woman may feel that he is unapproachable. She doesn't feel comfortable speaking her mind or ask-

ing for what she wants. This frustration will only continue to build.

8. **Uncommitted:** A woman may feel that he doesn't care about her needs. She needs to feel his personal commitment and enthusiasm, and although a man may feel this way when he is in his cave planning a solution, it will not show.

9. **Unresponsive:** A woman manager will feel as though a man is not being responsive to her direction or respecting her position. Coworkers may feel unsupported and resist giving support.

10. **Judgmental:** Female employees may feel as if they are in trouble or their jobs are in jeopardy, and panic. Ultimately, this will only create defensive behavior in others, because they will feel as though they are being unfairly judged.

11. **Angry:** A woman may feel as though a man is angry with her, or he doesn't want to talk with her because he doesn't like her.

12. **Desperate:** Women managers, employees, and customers may assume there is a big fire you are putting out, and the company is in big trouble. When people don't understand what is happening, they often assume the worst.

13. **Resentment:** A woman may conclude that a man has a list of resentments, and as a result has put up a wall of indifference. This will make her feel unfairly judged. As a result, she will be defensive or apprehensive.

14. **Dismissive:** When a man is in his cave, his attention goes to the biggest fire that needs to be put out. If a woman's problem is a little fire, he easily becomes distracted from her message. A woman may interpret this to mean that what she has to say isn't important to him or that she isn't important to him.

By occasionally reviewing this list of ways he may be misunderstood, a man will be motivated to demonstrate a more caring and considerate attitude. Seeing the wisdom in restraining his grumbles, he will soften his sharp edges with a little more small talk, warmth, and patience. Likewise, when women review this list, they can remember that men are from Mars and they may be misinterpreting his cave behaviors.

The Politics of Inclusion and Exclusion

When a woman views a man solving a problem in his cave, she may conclude that he is excluding her because he doesn't value her contribution. He suddenly seems unsupportive, inconsistent, and uncaring, when he is just trying to do his job. When we don't understand something, we often imagine the worst, particularly when our livelihood is at stake. Men are often misunderstood by women to be much more resistant or unsupportive than they are.

In a similar manner, when a man views a woman talking about a problem that could be solved alone, he assumes that she can't solve it on her own. He doesn't realize that she may already have a great solution in mind. Her sharing is simply to include others in the problem-solving process.

Let's explore a few examples to illustrate the workplace politics of inclusion and exclusion:

Karen is in sales. She receives a memo that sales are lagging in a particular state. Her first reaction is to talk about this new and unexpected problem with coworkers and her manager. After some talk with coworkers, she schedules a meeting with her manager and presents the problem.

Prior to the meeting, she concludes the solution is obvious. Since it is such a big problem, she feels the need to include Jerome, her manager. On Venus it would be rude to exclude another for such an important problem, even though the solution is somewhat obvious.

On Venus it would be rude to exclude another, even though the solution is obvious.

When she enters Jerome's office, she clearly has an idea about what needs to be done but doesn't immediately say so. She presents the problem and asks Jerome what he thinks should be done. He gives the obvious solution and she agrees it is a good idea. She then moves on to implement it.

She walks out of the meeting thinking she has proven how conscientious and competent she is. This, however, is not Jerome's perspective. After the meeting, Jerome quietly wonders, "Why did she come to me? What a waste of time. The solution was obvious. I'm not sure she is capable of doing this job."

This could have been avoided. When approaching her male manager, Karen needed to minimize the time she spent talking about the problem and instead let him know that she had a solution. Rather than ask Jerome for a solution, she needed to let him know the solution she came up with. This way Jerome gets a clear message that she is competent.

It is essential for women to remember that when dealing with men, it is best to talk less about the problem and more about the solution. If you don't get right to the solution, he will think you are unable to come up with one.

When dealing with men, it is best to talk less about the problem and more about the solution.

Let's turn the tables and imagine that Karen is the manager and Jerome has received notice that the sales are lagging.

Jerome is in sales. He receives a memo that sales are lagging in a particular state. He then drops everything to find a solution. When his manager, Karen, finds out that he has dropped other duties to put out this fire, she is displeased. She wonders, "Why didn't he come to me? Why didn't he ask for my help? How could he neglect these other responsibilities? I need to have a talk with him."

After their talk, Jerome feels unappreciated for taking the necessary initiative. Karen asks a lot of questions and Jerome feels as if he is getting the third degree and being treated like a third-grader. He reasons, "Why talk about it when we can be doing something about it?"

When women talk about a problem, a man reasons, Why talk about it when we can be doing something to solve it?

Instead of being rewarded for his independence, Jerome feels punished. Karen senses his resistance to her interest and contributions and concludes that he is not a team player and cannot be relied on. Instead of feeling more connected after this discussion, there is an unresolved underlying tension.

In this example, Jerome asserted himself to solve the problem. He did what would be respected on his planet but not on hers. Karen expected him to talk to her first to get help. Together, she thought, they would have come up with a solution that worked for everyone.

Jerome could have avoided the conflict. By taking time to let Karen know there was a problem in sales, that he was handling it, and that he would be happy to include her if she wanted to talk about it. A simple FYI (for your information) memo could have easily worked to describe the problem and solution.

The Advantages and Disadvantages
of Talking about Problems

Many communication problems can be resolved when both men and women understand how we approach solving problems differently. With this insight we are better equipped to determine when it is appropriate to talk about problems and when it is not.

On Venus, talking about problems is a way to feel better, but here on Earth where we work together it has many strong advantages and disadvantages. An awareness of both assists you in making the right choice for you in different settings:

1. **Advantage:** By including others in the discussion of a problem, a deeper awareness of the problem is developed. This increased awareness can sometimes create a clarity that makes the solution obvious. In this case, a meeting of minds can generate a more effective and efficient solution.

Disadvantage: By including others in the process of solving a problem, different points of view can create unnecessary conflict. Not only does it take more time, but it can give those who resist you the opportunity to join forces. While including others, unless all feel fully heard, feelings can be offended. Too many cooks cannot only create a greater possibility of conflict, but the process takes more time. This time factor becomes dramatically increased when people disagree with each other. All this can sometimes be avoided by simply doing what you think is best.

2. **Advantage:** By sharing the problem with others, you are insured of having their support in implementing your solution. In-

creasing an awareness of the problem motivates others to provide their help. This "goodwill" may also insure that this problem is not repeated in the future. By building up an awareness of the problem, others are motivated to support its solution.

Disadvantage: Involving others may motivate them to talk about their problems as well. Rather than getting their support, you can get their problems. The problem can become much bigger than it was, and a quick solution is no longer possible. Others may feel you are not appreciative of the many opportunities you have been given and withdraw their support.

Sometimes just the act of bringing in others to talk about a problem can make a problem appear much bigger than it really is. Before you know it, either you are making a mountain out of a mole hill or it just appears that way to others. Too much talk is often considered a waste of time by those who are in a hurry to get things done. You may be viewed as a problem maker rather than solver.

When a problem gets too big, sometimes nothing gets done. In this case, building up the problem just blocks its solution. Sometimes to motivate change, a problem needs to be broken down or minimized. Keeping problems small insures that a solution can be implemented.

When one small problem is solved, it motivates other similar problems to be solved as well. Instead of considering how to remove a whole wall, the process gets started by removing one brick and then another.

3. **Advantage:** Involving others to find a solution engages others and creates an increased motivation to participate in the solution. Skilled leaders know that the secret of motivating others to follow is to make them a part of the solution.

Disadvantage: Making others aware of your problems can weaken your image as a competent worker. As we have explored, sharing problems is viewed as a sign of weakness on

Mars. Those in competition with you will use this information to put you down and make you look weak and incompetent. They can attempt to prove they are more deserving for advancement and opportunity. Being open about problems makes you much more vulnerable to attack.

If you want to change lanes in traffic, the polite and lawful thing to do is put on your signal. In some cities, if you put on your blinkers to change lanes, the person in the other lane will speed up so you can't get in front of his car.

Likewise, the work world is competitive. When you sell less, they have the opportunity to look better. If you lose your expert status, they can step over you. Though this isn't the world we dream of creating, it is the way some people operate. The sea is filled with both dolphins and sharks that react in very different ways.

4. Advantage: Sharing the problem and the process of solving the problem increases a sense of community and connection between workers. This team-building process generates a greater sense of trust, collaboration, and cooperation in the workplace. Bringing together different points of view creates a synergy that can inspire greater creativity. More and more, companies are realizing the many values of approaching company problems with teams. This team spirit can also be generated by involving coworkers in athletic activities and challenges or retreats with many structured group activities.

Disadvantage: Familiarity breeds contempt. By sharing problems with others, a sense of equality is generated. If you have increased privileges or have made advances in the company, then jealousy arises. Instead of creating a warm feeling by sharing your problems, others with less privilege or rank in the company feel resentful. It seems unfair that they are more competent and yet have less status.

When a leader shares problems it can create division instead of unity. Followers need to feel their leader is in control, or else they might follow someone else. Sharing too many problems can create panic and frustration. Why should followers work hard? If their leader fails, they, too, will fail. To make the work worth the effort, it should always appear that great progress is being made.

5. **Advantage:** With more women in management, some men feel resentful and resist female authority. In a team activity, a man will gradually learn to respect this process as he experiences that better ideas sometimes do get generated when more minds are involved. When men understand the value of talking about problems, they will have greater respect for women and less resistance to following their leadership.

Disadvantage: On Mars they support those who appear to have the winning solution. To appear as if you don't have a solution makes you seem weak. To talk about problems is advertising your incompetence. When women in management positions are open about their problems, men view it as a sign of incompetence, lose respect, and resist and resent those women.

Teamwork

Teamwork is respected on Mars and Venus, but it has completely different meanings. On Mars, teamwork means everyone has his specific talents, duties, and departments. As a team, they work to support each other, but they don't share or switch positions. An offensive lineman doesn't even consider taking the position of a quarterback.

On Venus, teamwork means people share responsibilities, duties, and tasks. They do them together, and there is no clear or rigid distinction regarding who does what. They are more fluid and flexible. This egalitarian ideal of teamwork is very different from the Martian ideal. By understanding our differences, both men and women can more clearly respect the politics of inclusion and exclusion in their particular working environment.

An offensive lineman would not even consider taking the position of a quarterback.

When a woman has a solitary job or she happens to be in charge, she will need to feel she can talk about problems to get assistance in finding the right solution. Men will often misinterpret this need as a sign of weakness rather than a useful strategy for creative problem solving while also minimizing stress.

When a man is working in a collaborative environment, he still needs to have specific responsibilities for which he is fully accountable. To feel he has to talk about problems that come up without being able to take swift action to solve them will eventually wear him out. He particularly needs some arena, however small, where he is completely in charge, responsible, and accountable for creating results.

With an understanding of this difference, men and women can begin to be more considerate of their unique needs as they work together to achieve their goals. A woman does not have to sacrifice her need to collaborate and cooperate when she understands a man's need for cave time. A man doesn't have to sacrifice his need to solve problems independently when he realizes that women do not always demand collaboration but often just seek to be heard. He can still have his independent activities and create time to include women coworkers, managers, employees, customers, and clients.

6

Feelings in the Workplace

Both men and women have feelings, but how they express their feelings in the workplace is very different. When two people speak the same language, sharing feelings is a way to strengthen the bond of trust and connection. Communicating feelings, when done appropriately, can increase cooperation and confidence at all levels in the workplace. By building trust, productivity, and job satisfaction increase as stress and tension decrease.

Feelings are conveyed not just by words but by gestures, facial expressions, and tones. It is estimated that only twenty percent of communication involves the choice of words. While words are important, it is the communication of unspoken feelings that is more important. A happy smile, a delighted giggle, an understanding "mhum" sound, a confident tone of voice, or the nod of the head can be much more potent than a well-organized presentation. The feelings you convey will evoke similar feelings in others. Most decision makers will consider all the facts, figures, and logic, but when it comes to signing on the dotted line, a feeling or hunch makes or breaks the deal.

Sharing Feelings on Mars and Venus

On Mars, the sharing of positive feelings builds trust and respect, while on Venus, the sharing of *both* positive and negative feelings builds relationships. Men readily respect positive feelings like confidence, joy, satisfaction, pride, humor, happy relief, and relaxation, but they often don't respect negative feelings.

A man will tend to focus on expressing positive feelings rather than negative feelings. When he does express negative feelings, if he is to earn the respect of other men, he is careful to make sure they are expressed in a manner that is not personal. He may be frustrated, but he will not express "personal frustration." For example, he might indicate that he is frustrated that a delivery is late, but he will not show that he is frustrated because he is having a bad day.

When a man expresses negative feelings, instinctively they are expressed in an impersonal manner.

On Venus they don't favor positive or negative. Nothing is black or white.

For women, any feeling, positive or negative, expressed in a respectful manner can be an opportunity to share and connect with another. They do not discern between personal or impersonal emotions. There is no big taboo about revealing vulnerable feelings or negative emotions. Unlike men, they do not view expressing personal feelings as a form of weakness.

Personal versus Impersonal Feelings

It is easy to distinguish positive from negative feelings, but to separate personal and impersonal feelings takes some training. Most men automatically filter out their personal feelings but can freely express the nonpersonal ones. On the other hand, women tend to filter out impersonal feelings and freely express personal feelings. The problem that emerges from this difference is that men and women misinterpret each other and feel blamed.

Men automatically filter out their personal feelings but easily express nonpersonal ones.

Here are some examples of personal and impersonal feelings. In each example, the phrase "The letter was lost, I don't know what we are going to do" is expressed with a different emotion. While the emotion is the same, the meaning is different on Mars and Venus. This chart helps make clear the distinction between personal and impersonal reactions.

Impersonal Feelings	Personal Feelings
When he says, "The letter was lost. I don't know what we are going to do," he means:	When she says, "The letter was lost. I don't know what we are going to do," she means:
He is frustrated that the letter was lost and as a result an opportunity was missed.	She is frustrated that the letter was lost, she had asked for it, and now she feels that she is not being heard.
He is disappointed that sales were down in the third quarter.	She is disappointed that her efforts to improve sales were not implemented.

Impersonal Feelings	**Personal Feelings**
He is worried that the project will not be finished in time or he will not have time to do it.	She is worried that she will be blamed if the project is not finished in time and lose her job.
He is embarrassed that the work was not very good because the letter was lost.	She is embarrassed that others may see her as inefficient and uncaring.
He is angry because without the letter the job will not get finished.	She is angry because without the letter she may lose credibility.
He is sad because so much time was wasted and the project will not be recognized.	She is sad because she disappointed others and she wasted her time.
He is afraid because he does not know how they will make up the time lost.	She is afraid because she may lose respect from her peers.
He is sorry the letter was lost because the project will not get done in time.	She is sorry that the letter was lost and she feels powerless to do anything about it.
He is furious that the letter was lost because the other company will get the deal.	She is furious that the letter was lost because she worked so hard and to no avail. She may not get her promotion.
He is hurt because he worked hard on the project, and now it has failed.	She is hurt because she has worked hard on the project and her participation was not recognized.
He is scared that the company will look bad and not have another chance.	She is scared because the company looks bad and she now feels that she can't trust others in her department.

Impersonal Feelings	**Personal Feelings**
He is ashamed that the project failed and the company really looks bad.	She is ashamed that the project failed and now she looks very unprofessional.

In each of the above examples men and women tend to misunderstand each other. A man hears personal feelings as blaming statements, while a woman hears impersonal feelings as blaming statements.

Without an understanding of how men and women express emotions differently, women often feel attacked by men or take their emotional expressions personally when that is not how they are intended. Another man in the same situation would not take it personally. It is quite common for two men to argue with a lot of feeling in the tone of their voices, and neither feels personally attacked or gets personally defensive. A woman listening to the conflict may become alarmed, but men listening recognize that no one is being personally attacked and so all is OK. If it gets personal, then other men listening would feel the need to intervene to avoid escalating tension and conflict.

In a similar manner, when men hear women express their feelings in a more personal manner, although a woman would not feel attacked or blamed, a man will. The most well known example of this concerns anger. On a music album, Barbra Streisand popularized the message that men are respected when they express anger, but when women express anger they are seen in a negative light. She was correct. This is unfair for women, but fortunately there is a way to understand each other better.

Not all women who express anger are seen in this light. Some women who express their anger are seen as strong. When a man or woman is able to express anger in an impersonal manner, then men listen and respect what is being said. When a woman's anger is personal, resulting from her feeling personally attacked, hurt, or wounded, it is then that she is viewed in a negative light.

On Venus, there is nothing wrong with expressing personal feelings of anger, but on Mars it is heard as a personal attack.

**An angry woman is often seen in a negative light,
but an angry man tends to be respected more.**

When a woman's anger is personal, men mistakenly conclude that she is blaming others and taking no responsibility for what happened. When a woman's or man's anger is respected by men as an expression of strength and conviction, it is because the anger is about a situation or circumstance. Personal feelings in the workplace are often viewed by men with less respect.

What determines whether something is appropriate is the context in which it is expressed. If you are attempting to win the respect of someone from Mars, expressing personal emotions in the workplace is inappropriate because they can be so easily misunderstood and misinterpreted unless the man is adept in understanding Venusians (and most men are not). When a man hears women express personal feelings, the man often interprets their behaviors as selfish, self-pitying, or as finger-pointing. When women hear men express impersonal feelings, they often feel men are cold, inconsiderate, and indirectly blaming others.

In his Academy Award–winning role in the movie *As Good As It Gets*, Jack Nicholson explains how he is able to portray women so intimately: "I think about my male friends, take away all reason and sense of accountability, and I am left with how women think." Though this is not accurate, it is how many men, at times, misinterpret how women think and feel in the workplace. With a better understanding of our differences, this can be corrected. Understanding impersonal and personal feelings helps both men and women to see through the illusion of blame and more effectively realize our true intention to be more professional in the workplace.

Who's Blaming Who

One of the biggest problems with personal emotions in the workplace is that men tend to react defensively. When a man reacts defensively, his emotions become more personal, and he starts to blame others. In a similar manner, when a man expresses impersonal feelings, a woman will withdraw and react in a more impersonal manner. At this point, she will begin to blame him for his lack of sensitivity and consideration.

Men have personal feelings just like women, but as a general rule, unless he feels *extremely* mistreated, he will keep his personal feelings to himself. This is the Martian code of professionalism. It is similar to the idea that the customer is always right. To be professional, one doesn't think so much about oneself but focuses primarily on what it takes to get the job done and provide the best service.

On Venus, there is a similar but different code. As a general rule, unless a woman is feeling *extremely* mistreated, she will try to stay personal and not become impersonal. Blaming others is also considered inappropriate.

Many times men feel unfairly blamed and women claim they are not blaming. Women often say, "I am not blaming you, I am just telling you how I feel." Likewise, women claim a man is blaming when he is simply upset and explaining why he thinks he is right. As a result women feel "men just want to be right" and are therefore "unapproachable." A woman will conclude that a man cannot "hear her" when really he can hear much more than she thinks and will consider her comments.

Giving and Receiving Support

When a woman expresses personal emotions she is looking for support and giving it. Her openness to share personal emotions is a sign of her willingness to trust another. At such times, a man can make a few small adjustments and strengthen the bond of trust in their working relationship.

A man does not instinctively give reassurance, because when he expresses his negative emotions he is not looking for emotional reassurance. For example, when he is disappointed, he doesn't want to hear a woman empathetically saying, "I know you must feel really disappointed." On his planet this kind of support is considered demeaning and condescending. At best it would make him feel uncomfortable, but most of the time it would be offensive.

Yet these same words could make most women feel supported. Let's look at a variety of ways a man or woman could respond to personal emotions in a supportive manner. When a man correctly identifies the tone of a woman's emotions without distancing himself, she already feels supported. By adding a supportive, reassuring comment, she feels even more support. Let's look at a few examples.

Giving Reassurance on Venus

**When a woman says, "The letter was lost. I don't know
what to do": Different personal emotions and
corresponding meaning are listed in column one; a
corresponding reassuring response is listed in column two.**

She feels:	How he can give reassurance:
Her tone is frustration. She is frustrated that the letter was lost; she had asked for it, and now she feels that she is not being heard.	He says, "This must be so frustrating, you had specifically asked for that letter . . . maybe next time they will listen to you."

She feels:	How he can give reassurance:
Her tone is disappointment. She is disappointed since her efforts to improve sales were not implemented.	He says, "It must be very disappointing, you had so many good ideas, and they just didn't listen . . . maybe now things will change."
Her tone is worry. She is worried that she will be blamed if the project is not finished in time and lose her job.	He says, "Are you worried about keeping your job? Everyone is so upset about this. Even if it doesn't finish on time, everyone knows it wasn't your fault . . . you are doing a good job."
Her tone is embarrassment. She is embarrassed that others may see her as inefficient and uncaring.	He says, "You seem embarrassed. It wasn't your fault. We know how much you care and put into this project."
Her tone is anger. She is angry, because without the letter she may lose credibility.	He says, "You have every right to be angry about this. I know it certainly is not your fault. It is so unfair . . . you have done a great job."
Her tone is sadness. She is sad, because she thought it would have turned out better, but instead she wasted her time.	He says, "It makes me sad, too. I know you thought it was going to turn out better. You did your best, and that's all you can ever do."
Her tone is fear. She is afraid, because she may not have enough time to correct the situation, and others will be disappointed in her.	He says, "I can understand if you are afraid. Everything is happening at once . . . I think it's going to be OK."
Her tone is regret. She is sorry that the letter was lost and feels powerless to do anything about it.	He says, "I know you feel sorry. No one expects you to make it reappear magically . . . it's OK."

She feels:

Her tone is outrage. She is furious that the letter was lost, because she worked so hard and to no avail; she may not get her promotion.

Her tone is hurt. She is hurt because she has worked hard on the project, and someone else may get the deal.

Her tone is anxious. She is scared that the company looks bad and she now feels she can't trust others in her department.

Her tone is shame. She feels bad that the project failed, and now she looks very unprofessional.

How he can give reassurance:

He says, "I would be furious, too. You have worked so hard and then this. I can appreciate how much you have done and how difficult this must be for you . . . you still deserve a promotion."

He says, "It must really hurt a lot. You worked so hard and now you may lose the deal. You didn't deserve this . . . I know it will eventually work out."

He says, "This is scary. Everyone is so busy. How can you trust anyone to remember anything? . . . Things will get better."

He says, "I know you feel really bad. You did all anyone could do. No one expects perfection . . . you handled this whole project in a very professional and competent manner."

At times of distress, a Venusian appreciates that someone else knows what she is going through and cares. On Venus, when you really care for someone, their joy makes you happy, and their sadness makes you sad. This matching of emotional tone makes your message assuring. In addition, by making a few validating comments and acknowledging statements, a woman will feel even more support.

Assurance is given by matching
a woman's emotional tone.

These same comments could easily backfire when talking to a Martian. On Mars, they assess themselves based on their competence. To offer help when he has not asked for it is to convey the message that he is somehow weak. Most of the time a man doesn't want a reassuring comment. His feelings are not personal, but impersonal, and require a different kind of support.

At such times, a man supports another man by not directly offering any reassuring comments or direct empathy. Instead he gives a special kind of encouragement. This is done in a manner that allows him to save face. This encouragement recognizes that he is somewhat distressed, and trusts in his ability to handle the situation in the best possible manner. Venusian reassuring comments can easily be interpreted as a lack of trust or criticism implying he can't handle the situation without her emotional support.

On Mars, reassuring comments can
easily be interpreted as a lack of trust.

On Mars, it is a mistake to directly acknowledge impersonal negative feelings. To a certain extent, these feelings are to be overlooked or ignored. Putting attention on his feelings gives the problem more importance, thus increasing the sense of failure. For most men, it would be completely inappropriate to say, "I know you must be hurting, let me help you."

Responding in the emotional tone of another in distress works on Venus, but not on Mars. If a man is disappointed, it doesn't work to feel disappointed "for him." If he is worried, don't express the tone of worry for him. When he is happy, you can feel happy for him, but when he is sad, it's not appropriate to feel sad for him. That can make him feel worse.

Often men don't even understand this. They just know that

after a woman expresses empathy they just want to shake it off. This explains why men don't share feelings with women and also why men have no idea how to give an empathetic comment.

This does not mean that all men will be turned off by emotional reassurance, but when they seem to pull away, a woman can correctly assess the situation. It is not that he doesn't want her support, it is that he doesn't want emotional empathy. With this insight she will not take his withdrawal personally. She can then easily undo her mistake with a simply apology. She could simply say, "Excuse me for getting so emotional." The less said the better.

One little apology can quickly mend the mistake. Without this understanding, a woman would never even consider giving an apology for either getting emotional or being empathetic. In this manner she can make light of it and give a brief apology. He will be able to easily let it go or release any resistance he has to her.

Giving Encouragement on Mars

Just as women appreciate reassurance at stressful times, a man will appreciate encouragement. Men love being appreciated and cheered on. To acknowledge what a man does encourages him on. If he is under stress and expressing negative emotions, there are ways a woman can be most supportive by making comments that sound encouraging on Mars.

An encouraging response, unlike a reassuring response, gives the message "I trust you can handle this, you clearly don't need my help." An encouraging message on Mars contains trust, acceptance, and appreciation.

An encouraging response, unlike a reassuring response, gives the message "I trust you can handle this alone."

   Keep in mind that the words alone are not enough. The tone
is very important. To give encouragement, make sure the tone is
not an empathetic, "I feel your pain" tone. It needs to be more
upbeat, sometimes jovial. Empathy tends to have a heavy tone,
while encouragement has a light tone. Imagine you were responding to the world's greatest expert. The last thing you would
do is "feel sorry" for him. Let's look at some examples.

He feels:	She can say to support:
He is frustrated that the letter was lost and as result an opportunity was missed.	She says in a tone of relief, "I'm sure glad I don't have to do your job."
He is disappointed that sales were down in the third quarter.	She says in a neutral tone, "Sometimes you win, sometimes you lose."
He is worried that the project will not be finished in time, or he will not have time to do it.	She says with a confident tone, "I'm not worried, you'll figure out something."
He is embarrassed that the work was not very good, because the letter was lost.	She says with a casual tone, "Well, you can't win them all."
He is angry, because without the letter he can't prove his competence.	She says in a playful tone, "Well, I guess that's why they pay you the big bucks."
He is sad, because so much time was wasted and he will have to start over.	She says in a matter-of-fact tone, "You can only do what you can do."
He is afraid, because he does not know how they will make up the time lost.	She says in a hopeful tone, "It's not over till it's over."

He feels:	She can say to support:
He is sorry the letter was lost, because the project will not get done in time.	She says in a carefree tone, "Well, it won't be the end of the world."
He is furious that the letter was lost, because the other company will get the deal.	She says in a tone of happy relief, "I'm sure glad I didn't lose that letter."
He is hurt, because he worked hard on the project and now it has failed.	She says in a relaxed tone, "You'll survive."
He is scared that the company will look bad and not have another chance.	She says in a trusting tone, "We'll get another break."
He is ashamed that the project will not succeed and the company really looks bad.	She says in an accepting tone, "Well, mistakes happen. That's life."

By role-playing and giving this kind of playful, matter-of-fact encouragement, a woman can learn to give the kind of support a man appreciates. By experiencing her resistance to this kind of support, she can begin to glimpse the kind of resistance men have to making reassuring gestures that are appreciated on Venus.

Expressing Feelings in the Workplace

The best way to stand out in the workplace is by expressing positive feeling. When you are confident, people have greater confidence in you. When you feel good about yourself and your job then others feel good being around you. When you feel calm then you are an oasis of peace and others will be drawn to you.

When you are able to appreciate the opportunities before you then you naturally attract more.

When you feel good about yourself and your job then others feel good being around you.

Feelings can be shared directly with words, but most often and most powerfully they are shared through the tone of your voice and your physical mannerisms. For example, after completing a task, there is big difference between a "big sigh of relief" and a "big sigh of exasperation." The actual behavior of taking a deep breath is the same, but the feeling conveyed through the tone and facial expression is entirely different. A sigh could convey positive feelings, neutral feelings, or negative feelings.

Here is a short list of how men may misinterpret negative emotions:

Shared Negative Feelings	**Shared Negative Feelings**
Martian Misinterpretation	**Martian Misinterpretation**
She expresses regret and embarrassment.	He may hear she failed and is inadequate.
She expresses worry and fear.	He may hear she is insecure, helpless, or weak.
She expresses hurt, disappointment, and sadness.	He may hear she is blaming others for her problems.
She expresses frustration, anger, and resentment.	He may hear she is feeling sorry for herself or complaining when she could be doing something.

Containing Negative Feelings

On Mars negative feelings are a sign of weakness and are processed privately. Healthy men have a healthy sense of privacy regarding their inner demons. When personal feelings of frustration, anger, disappointment, etc., arise, he skillfully holds back or contains these feelings until a later time when he can process and release them. This is often accomplished by doing something that is fun, relaxing, or challenging that is not directly work-related. Once he feels more relaxed and peaceful he is able to casually reflect once again on what happened at work from a more positive perspective.

Unmannered, weak, insecure, or dysfunctional men will readily display negative emotions and as a result will be subjected to the same disrespect that a woman would. On Mars a professional is someone who can do the job regardless of what he is feeling inside. In show business this is reflected in the popular expression "The show must go on."

> **On Mars, a professional is someone who can do their job regardless of what they are feeling inside.**

When it comes to expressing negative feelings in the workplace, both men and women are judged by men with the same set of rules. The inability to contain negative emotions is unprofessional. When men, not just women, are unable to contain negative feelings they lose the respect of other men. Unless a man has some special talent that makes him indispensable, an inability to contain negative emotions will block his success.

One important distinction in this example is that on Venus, healthy and well-mannered women do not have this sense of privacy regarding their inner negative emotions. On their planet it is not offensive to display negative emotions. To the contrary, it is a symptom of healthy self-esteem. As we have already explored, sharing negative feelings on Venus is an efficient way to minimize stress while strengthening connections and building trust.

**On Venus it is not offensive to
express negative emotions.
To the contrary, it is a symptom of healthy self-esteem.**

On Venus, however, a woman will discern when and with whom she will share her feelings. Strong women, like men, also have the capacity to contain negative emotions. A well-mannered Venusian doesn't readily share her negative feelings with someone who is not her friend or supporter. She will often contain them until the right time and place. When she feels more trusting she will begin to open up and share. This explains why sometimes you can ask a woman what's wrong when clearly something is bothering her, but she will insist it is nothing.

**When you ask a woman what's wrong when clearly
something is bothering her, she may insist it is nothing.**

A woman, however, will mean, "Something is wrong but I don't know if this is the right time to talk about it. If you care and you have the time, then ask more questions and I will tell more."

In this example the difference between men and women is that when a man says "nothing is wrong," he is not only containing his feelings but he doesn't want to talk about them.

Making this shift toward containing negative emotions is actually not such a stretch for women. A woman is not required to deny her fundamental feminine nature. Women are already experts in "containing" feelings in situations where they don't feel supported. To succeed in the workplace she can now apply this same skill and "contain" her feelings to more successfully give support. With this insight, instead of wondering why she is losing the respect and support of men, she can do something about it.

By applying the discipline and restraint necessary to give support, both men and women can learn to contain their negative emotions and reactions in the workplace. This on Mars is called professional behavior. Some women mistakenly conclude this is unhealthy when it is actually a healthy discipline for both men and women. It would only be unhealthy if a woman didn't take time outside the workplace to decharge her stress. Suppressing feelings is unhealthy but "containing" feelings and then dealing with them at a later time outside the workplace is very healthy.

Besides creating more success, containing negative emotions exercises the muscles of emotional control. When you practice holding back and then freely expressing emotion, at an appropriate time, then you gain a greater control of them. This increases your ability to manage stress. Instead of letting your emotions control you, you gradually learn to control them.

Instead of letting your emotions control you, contain your feelings and learn to control them.

Because it is helpful to take time to explore upsetting feelings in therapy, people mistakenly conclude they should do this in the workplace. The workplace is not, nor should it be, therapeutic. Likewise, it is inappropriate to use business time to support your own personal needs to process your emotional distress. By making sure that you have a personal life outside of your work life, you will have the time and support needed to handle "contained" emotions.

If one is not getting the emotional support they need from their personal life outside the office then they should look to a therapist and not their job for that kind of support. Learning to contain upset feelings and then taking time to process them at a later time is one of the healthiest things a person can learn to do.

**Processing negative feelings at a later time is one of the
healthiest things a person can learn to do.**

This adjustment of containing feelings is like a new kind of
makeup to bring out a woman's best characteristics in the workplace. Holding it in this light is helpful because some women resist having to hide a part of themselves, when the truth is they
are already doing it in many ways. Many women willingly put
on makeup to hide a blemish, put caps on their teeth or use
whiteners, or wear clothes that will particularly flatter their figure. Containing negative emotions is just another way a woman
can accentuate her best characteristics.

This doesn't mean she can't be herself. It just means she cannot be all of herself all of the time. Successful people have
learned how to authentically express different parts of themselves at different times. They understand that you can't express
all of who you are at all times. There is, however, a time and
place for each part of who you are.

**Successful people learn how to authentically express
different parts of themselves at different times.**

It is not just women but men as well who are required to hold
back from freely expressing whatever they feel. Men are generally more receptive to this idea because they have to work on it
all the time. Although women are often seen as more emotional,
it is not an accurate generalization. Differences in one's tendency
to react emotionally are based on different temperaments and
are not gender-specific. What is different between men and
women is how we process emotions differently.

Men have a much greater tendency to act without thinking
when they experience negative emotions. A man in combat may
feel enormous fear but he learns to contain his fear and not act
on it by running away. He contains his anger and ensures that he

doesn't act impulsively. He learns to contain his sadness and get the job done regardless of how he feels. Men are already more familiar with the need to contain feelings, and so with the added awareness of what women need they can more easily put it into practice.

When men and women take time to process their contained feelings at home or in more personal relationships it is easier to make this adjustment in the workplace. When, however, there is no outlet for feelings in our personal life this small adjustment can seem impossible.

7

Why Men Don't Listen . . . or Do They?

One of the biggest obstacles men face in earning the trust of women is their attitude toward achieving the bottom line. In the workplace, a man is often so task-oriented and focused that he will dispense with all small talk and give the impression that he doesn't care about the people with and for whom he works. He may care about producing the best product or providing the best price, but if he doesn't succeed in communicating that he cares about people, he may lose trust and support. Instead of being recognized as someone you can depend on, he will lose her trust.

By not taking more time to listen a man gives the impression that he really doesn't care enough. The way men communicate often gives the impression to women that they are not hearing or validating their needs and wishes. Although he may be competent to solve a problem, she will not be able to recognize or appreciate his abilities. The number-one way men sabotage their success in working with women is by not taking enough time to demonstrate caring and consideration.

One of the biggest obstacles women face in earning the respect of men is their attitude regarding business interactions in the workplace. When a woman takes things personally and feels hurt, excluded, rejected, unappreciated, or offended by typical Martian behavior, she alienates herself. As a result, she is seen as the problem and not part of the solution. Instead of being treated in a personal manner with compassion and empathy, she is sometimes unfairly viewed as an obstacle.

For Martians, it is as if she is creating problems that do not exist. An old Martian saying that women need to know is "To take offense is to offend." The number-one way women sabotage their success and alienate a man is to take offense or respond personally to his actions and behaviors. Even if his actions are personal, to react as if they are not will diffuse the tension.

> **An old Martian saying woman need to know is**
> **"To take offense is to offend."**

By learning to interpret male workplace behavior, a woman can learn not to take things personally that would normally hurt or offend on her planet. When she is not feeling hurt, disrespected, or rejected by men, men will be more accepting and appreciative of her.

Without understanding our differences, men unknowingly do things that a woman takes personally. She then offends him back by taking offense. The most potent way men offend women is by not listening or responding the way women expect. At all levels and areas of the workplace, men respond to women in an impersonal manner, and women take it personally.

At times when a woman feels personally ignored, attacked, or minimized, his resistance is often just about getting the job done.

With this perspective on how men think and behave, it is easier to accept, ignore, overlook, or even laugh about behaviors that used to be annoying or threatening. On Mars, business is business and not personal.

How Men Inadvertently Lose Business

The most significant way men appear too impersonal is in the way they listen or don't listen. A woman takes it personally when she concludes that a man doesn't care about her. The message she gets is that she is not important. Let's explore a few examples.

A promising high-tech company was preparing to go public. Although the bottom line was profitable, they needed a known name to inspire confidence in the management. Of the many applicants, Richard Adkins was favored by board members to become president of the company. He had started, developed, and sold a similar company with a personal profit to him of three hundred million dollars. On Mars, and to the men on the board, his credentials alone made him best for the job.

The company was based on a product line developed by a woman scientist, Linda Tompkins, who was the CEO. It was her company, and the board needed her approval to appoint the new president. The male members of the board were totally impressed by his interview, but Linda would have nothing to do with him. If Richard had understood Venusians, he would have been able to make a much better impression. The behavior that impressed the men on the board created mistrust in the CEO.

During his interview, she told him how their company was different and that they had many unique challenges. Richard responded to her sentences with confident comments like, "I understand that. We can do this. . . ."

He had complete confidence and a résumé to back it up. For every concern she expressed, he had an answer. His clarity and focus on solutions were impressive to the men but frustrating and even offensive to her. After fifteen minutes of his solutions, a wall went up inside her, and she would have nothing to do with him. When she later rejected him for the job, all of the men and Richard were baffled.

A man's clarity, confidence, and focus on solutions is impressive to the men but frustrating to women.

In this example, Richard generated immediate trust with the men by giving quick and confident solutions. By giving quick solutions instead of listening more, he failed to build trust with Linda. All he needed to do was slow down and take more time to listen, ponder, and ask more questions about the problem. By taking more time to consider the uniqueness of their situation, he would have established a greater sense of connection, relationship, and rapport.

Men are assured by confidence and quick answers but women trust a man who understands her particular problems. Linda could not trust Richard's confidence because she knew he didn't know their particular problems and challenges in the market. She knew this with certainty, because she had not yet expressed them all and this man thought he had all the answers. Linda felt that he was arrogant, condescending, and didn't care about what she had to say. She was not about to do business with someone who didn't listen.

The Benefits of Listening

Demonstrating that you care on Venus has more to do with how you listen and respond than with what you say and do. Most men don't have a clue what women are talking about when women feel, think, or say men don't listen. Here are ten benefits of learning to listen in a way that makes Venusians feel heard:

1. When you listen to a woman and do not rush to the point, she will feel you care and will give you her trust. This increases her willingness to do business with you or work harmoniously.

2. When you ask questions of a woman to gather more information, she will feel more engaged or drawn out and as a result more motivated to do business with you.

3. By not interrupting a woman's discussion with solutions, you will acknowledge the validity of her problems so that she can trust the validity of your solutions.

4. By reflecting on what she has said, you help to clarify her thinking, and then she will appreciate you more. With greater clarity, she is able to give you more trust and support.

5. By listening to her objections without interruption, you communicate the intention to be of service and make her feel safe. As a result, she can be more decisive in making a purchase or agreement.

6. If you remember what she has said and ask related questions, she will know that you are capable of responding to her needs. She will feel assured in depending on your services.

7. When you hear her frustration, worry, and disappointment without minimizing her feelings with an immediate explanation or excuse, she will begin to appreciate you. By relating in some way to her feelings you will build rapport, which strengthens trust in any work relationship.

8. By not offering a solution right away when a woman talks about problems, you make a woman feel respected, because her competence in solving the problem is not being minimized. She feels validated and is more eager to receive your services and support.

9. By listening to a list of complaints and problems with patience, a man appears more confident to a woman. She trusts that he is a "can-do" person and feels assured that he values her and is not just interested in the bottom line. This builds rapport.

10. Listening to a woman with empathy will give comfort. She will feel she can count on you. She will support you and refer your services to all her friends.

Learning to Listen on Venus

The primary reason women take things personally is that they don't feel heard. As women begin to recognize that men are oblivious to how women interpret situations, it makes it easier for a woman not to take things so personally.

If someone were to come into your china shop and start breaking things, you would feel disrespected. If a bull was wandering through narrow aisles and knocking things over, you wouldn't feel offended. In a similar manner, if you understand a man is a bull in a china shop, the work world doesn't seem as cold, disrespectful, and heartless. In most cases, when a man seems not to be listening, it is not an expression of disrespect on his planet. He would treat his best friend in the same way.

> **When it comes to Venusian feelings,**
> **a Martian is a bull in a china shop.**

When women say men don't listen, they can mean many things. The following list can help a man understand how she feels when he doesn't listen. The list can also help women understand why a man thinks he does listen and she thinks he doesn't. Let's explore twelve common reasons women don't feel heard and take offense.

1. When a Man Ignores a Woman

A woman feels a man is not listening when he simply ignores what she is saying. In the middle of the conversation he will look off or think about something else. When he brings his attention back, he will say, "What did you say?" or "Would you say that again?" This seems disrespectful to a woman and is evidence that he wasn't listening. From his perspective, he lost his focus for a few moments and has now come back. On Mars, his questioning is evidence that he cares and is interested.

When a woman cares about someone, she doesn't think about other things when he or she talks. A sign of her caring is that she isn't distracted. So when a man is easily distracted, she concludes that he doesn't care about her.

When a man is easily distracted, a woman concludes that he doesn't care about her.

His tendency to get distracted may have nothing to do with her but with the way in which she is communicating. When a man is under stress, if she is not getting right to the point, his mind will drift, and he may tend to think of other things more pressing or urgent to him. For a woman, this behavior is a sign of disrespect. She cannot even conceive of behaving that way in an important work relationship. Another man would not take it personally and would instinctively realize that this man must be under a lot of stress and pressure. When a man gets distracted, a woman can only conclude that she is unimportant to him if she doesn't understand men are from Mars.

When a man temporarily ignores her, he doesn't even know that he is ignoring her. His mind is elsewhere, focused on solving a problem. As a result, she feels he is ignoring her and he doesn't even know he is doing it. With this insight, a man can make a concerted effort to stay focused on what she is saying and not drift away. In this example, when women think "men don't listen," it is more accurate to conclude he was listening but not giving his full attention.

2. When a Man Gives a Solution

A woman feels a man is not listening when he gives her a solution to her problem before she has finished talking about it. He thinks he knows the problem she wants solved, but from her point of view, he doesn't, because she hasn't expressed it yet. Women often talk about the bigger picture before they get down to the specific point or problem that needs to be solved. Men don't realize this because when a man talks about a problem, he begins by focusing on what he seeks to solve. A man thinks he is a good listener because, right away, he could give a good solution.

When a man rushes to give his solution, he assumes that he has heard her and is responding to her need. When she says he doesn't listen, it doesn't make sense to him, because he did listen before offering his solution. He does not know that the problem he thinks he is solving for her relates only to a small portion of what she has to say. By offering a quick solution, he is not giving her what she wants. On Mars, his immediate solution is seen as evidence of his competence, but on Venus it implies disrespect. Whenever a woman talks, before she wants a solution she wants first to be heard. She cannot trust his solution if he doesn't first hear the complete problem with all its facets.

On Venus, they express a series of ideas before they get to the real issue they want to discuss.

When women think "men don't listen," it is more accurate to conclude that a man did listen but not to everything she wanted to say. This reaction will make more sense to him and she will feel less minimized. Women greatly appreciate Mr. Fix-It, but only after she feels *fully* heard.

3. *When a Man Assumes She Needs a Solution*

A woman feels a man is not listening when he gives her a solution when she is not asking for one. She just wants him to be aware of the problem for which she is going to suggest a solution. When he gives a solution it seems as if he doesn't think she can come up with a solution. He knows he listened because he offered a good solution. When a woman thinks "men don't listen," it is more accurate to conclude he did listen but assumed she didn't have a solution.

It is essential for women to take notice when a man thinks this way. Unless she does something to prevent it, he will conclude that she is incompetent or he may make her appear incompetent to others. When he starts to give a solution in front of others, she needs to respond quickly with something to indicate she has a solution. She could save face by saying, "I have a similar solution to suggest, but first I want to make sure everyone is aware of the problem."

Ideally, she could avoid this kind of problem by beginning a presentation with some kind of comment letting others know in advance she has a solution. She could say, "I have an effective plan of action to suggest, but first I want to make sure everyone is aware of the problem."

If a woman is in a private meeting with her manager or boss and he gives a suggestion before she gives her solution, she could say in a very friendly, matter-of-fact manner, "Oh, I've already worked out a solution. I just wanted you to be aware of the problem."

If he gives the solution she was already prepared to present, then she could say, "I also think we should handle it this way. I have talked to sales and they agree . . ."

In this way, after the fact, she makes it clear that she already had a solution by mentioning a few extra details of her legwork to develop what he might think was his solution. A man will respect that she has attempted to find a solution before bringing the problem to him.

On Mars, talking about problems can easily sound like whining and complaining.

When a man offers a solution, it is important to realize that he really didn't know that she already had a solution. When a man talks about a problem, he lets you know right away that he has a solution by getting right away to his solution. If a woman doesn't reveal her solution toward the beginning of a conversation, a man mistakenly concludes she is unable to solve the problem. This seems condescending to her, and once again she takes it personally. With this insight into the way men and women communicate about problems differently, a woman does not have to take it personally.

4. When a Man Forgets to Do Something

A woman feels a man is not listening when he forgets what she has asked him to do. She concludes that he didn't listen to her instead of accepting that he just forgot. When women think men don't listen, it is more accurate to conclude he listened but forgot what she wanted or that it was not at the top of his priorities.

Remembering requests is very important on Venus. Men don't mind if you forget the little things as long as you remember the big things or produce big results. Women, on the other hand, feel that remembering the little things indicates that they are important. On Venus, remembering the little things builds trust that you can and will do the big things. A woman translates what a man does in personal terms. Remembering to do the little things makes her feel you respect her.

When men forget to do the little things,
a woman will take it personally.

If a man forgets to do something little but remembers what
was most urgent or important, another man understands that the
little things were overlooked in the process. He does not take it
personally or even care. Women are different. When someone is
important to them, remembering the little things is just as important as the big things. In this way, a woman nurtures the personal side of the work relationship.

Often a woman feels overwhelmed in the workplace, simply
because everything matters to her. She is attempting to do all the
big things and little things. Some men judge this tendency as a
sign of incompetence. Though another woman would appreciate
this woman's caring attempt to do it all, a man will judge the behavior as an inability to prioritize what is most important. A
woman working with lots of men can relax more by realizing
this difference.

On Mars, forgetting to do the little things is not
a problem as long as the big things are being addressed.

A woman might stay up all night to do something that a man
forgot to do because he considered that it was not urgent or
pressing. From his perspective her effort was a waste, and thus
he doesn't have an authentic appreciation for what she has done.
She thinks she has helped out or done something worthy of acknowledgment. He wishes she would have gotten more sleep and
been in a better mood.

Often men conclude that women are unable to prioritize. This
is not correct. Women prioritize but their priorities are different. A
man instinctively prioritizes the bottom line and a woman prioritizes the quality of work relationships. Success in the workplace
today can be achieved only by a skillful blend of these sometimes

conflicting values. Many Venusian instincts work well for female relationships but not on Mars. The awareness of why men forget will help a woman not to take things personally and will allow her to do less without the fear of being judged.

5. When a Man Does What He Wants

A woman feels a man is not listening when he doesn't do what she has asked him to do. When he follows his own inner guidance or gut instincts, she may feel that he didn't listen to her. From his perspective, he listened but did what he thought was right. In this context, when women think "men don't listen," it is more accurate to conclude he listened but did not do what she wanted him to do.

With an attitude that says "men don't listen," a woman sounds like a disapproving mother telling her uncooperative boy to listen to her. When a child or dog is not obedient, women say he didn't listen. In a similar manner, when women say a man didn't listen, it has a condescending and demeaning tone, as if he is being compared to a disobedient child or dog.

> **When women say a man didn't listen, it has a condescending and demeaning tone.**

On Mars, what women might consider disobedience is considered to be assertiveness. A man often earns great respect by taking the risk to follow his gut instincts and do his own thing. It is a risk. If his gut instinct has proved to be effective, producing the desired results, he is a hero, but if he fails, he is irresponsible. He is not judged for his disobedience but by the results of his disobedience.

A man in a higher position of authority will excuse the defiance if he gets a result. If he fails, he will suffer a consequence. The penalty is measured by the lack of results.

Women alienate men by complaining that a man did not listen or that he wasn't obedient. A man reacting to this complaint may think, "Well, maybe he thought of something better to do." To avoid this reaction, a woman can instead focus on his lack of results. By not focusing on his lack of obedience, or complaining that he doesn't listen, she demonstrates that she is not taking it personally or putting herself above the bottom line.

6. When a Man Is Not Empathetic

A woman feels a man is not listening when he doesn't offer the empathetic response a woman would commonly give. Just because a man doesn't respond with empathy doesn't mean he didn't listen to what she said. He just may not relate to her feelings or express support the way a woman would. In this case, when women think "men don't listen," it is more accurate to conclude they listened but did not give an empathetic response.

It is important that she correctly interpret his reaction and not take it personally. He may hear her feelings, but on his planet, men minimize emotional distress as a way of displaying confidence in another and their ability to solve the problem. Rather than assume that he doesn't care or is indifferent, she can now remember that he doesn't know how to express empathy on Venus.

7. When a Man Interrupts a Woman

A woman feels a man is not listening when he interrupts her in the middle of her conversation. Men often interrupt each other to make a point and never feel as if the other person was not listening, particularly if the interruption was a good point or a relevant correction or argument. The relevance of the comment proves he was listening. When women think "men don't listen," in this instance it is more accurate to conclude he listened but was not polite in letting her finish.

Men communicate with different rules. It is similar to basket-ball. The objective is to get the ball in the hoop. Players will throw it back and forth until one shot gets it. No one minds when a player hogs the ball if his shots go in. It's only a problem if his shots don't go in. If a man interrupts to make a point, and he is on target, the last thing he would conclude is that he was impolite or disrespectful. She feels offended, and he is wondering why he is not getting points. He expects her to say something like, "Good point." She expects him to apologize.

**When a man interrupts he mistakenly expects a woman
to say something like, "Good point."**

A man can refrain from interrupting a woman if he knows it is expected of him. Once again, it is like basketball. There are times when a player gets a free throw. They take all the time they want and no one interferes. When communicating, if a woman doesn't feel comfortable bouncing ideas back and forth, she can directly say in a friendly tone, "Give me a few minutes to explain this fully and then tell me what you think." There is no need to demand this or request it in a firm tone. He is happy to listen in this way, he just needs to know what is expected of him. This lit-tle request can make a world of difference. If he interrupts again, then once again, in a friendly tone, say, "OK, OK, I'll let you know when I'm done and then you tell me what you think."

This friendly, accepting approach goes over much better than feeling resentful because he is not listening. Below are eight com-mon expressions women use when feeling the resentment of not being heard. Attitude is everything. Even these expressions would work fine if she delivered them humorously without a tone of resentment. To get a sense of how a man hears these comments, imagine a woman is feeling excluded and resentful and then makes any of the following comments:

1. Can I *just* finish?

2. Can I say *anything* around here?

3. Let *me* say something.

4. I *just* want to finish my point.

5. You're *not* listening.

6. You're *not* hearing me.

7. I can't say *anything*.

8. You *don't* understand.

When a woman makes such comments with a resentful tone a man will become defensive. From his perspective, he is listening and she can interrupt back at any time to make her point. He feels as if she is calling a foul, and he is playing by the rules. Without this understanding, men and women become adversarial rather than supportive.

Ideally, the best response from a woman when she feels interrupted is not to take it personally and simply to interrupt back in a friendly way and continue her point. The easy way to do this is to listen a little, compliment him, and then continue saying what she wanted to say. She could say, "Good idea, but . . ." or "All right, let me try saying this differently."

There is a big difference between saying, "You are not listening" and "All right, let me try saying this differently." Although the message is really the same, the second message is nonaccusatory and is clearly a sign that she has not taken his interruption personally.

8. *When a Man Finishes Her Sentence*

A woman feels a man is not listening when he finishes her sentence. When men do this for other men, they don't mind at all.

They get the message that he completely understands, which after all is the purpose of communicating in the first place. He could not complete the sentence if he wasn't listening and understanding. If a women feels a man is not listening when he is able to finish her sentence, it makes no sense to him. Men need to realize that a woman doesn't want him to finish her sentences. In this case, when women think "men don't listen," it is more accurate to conclude he listened but not in the way she wanted. He finished her sentence to convey his understanding.

A woman feels heard not just when her idea is understood, but because she has fully expressed herself. Although it may be reasonable on Mars to finish sentences for others, it is not on Venus. On Venus the act of her saying the words will often lead a woman to a place of greater understanding. The action of self-expression helps her to understand herself better, and in that process her ideas may change in midstream and become more enriched. When he breaks her flow by finishing her sentence, it can be disorienting to her and blocks her creative expression.

The act of self-expression helps a woman understand herself better.

Although it seems to him that he is expressing his understanding of what she has said, it doesn't have that impact. To her it says, "I already know what you are going to say so don't bother telling me." A woman will tend to feel disrespected because she knows that she is probably going to say more than just the point he is about to make. He may think he knows where she is going, but he can't because sometimes she is not fully sure until it comes out. This way of thinking and expressing is different on Mars. Men usually think about what they are going to say and then stick to it; women get an inspiration and go with the flow. In the process they discover where exactly they want to go.

9. When a Man Presumes to Know What a Woman Wants

A woman feels a man is not listening when he presumes to know what she wants when she hasn't made up her mind. A man will listen and conclude what she wants. Just because he comes to the wrong conclusion doesn't mean he wasn't listening. He thinks he is helping by reflecting back what he hears her asking for. Although this is acceptable on Mars, it can be rude and sound too "pushy" on Venus. In this example, when women think "men don't listen," it is more accurate to conclude he listened but was incorrect in presuming to know what she wanted.

Another similar mistake men make is to assume a woman needs his help to decide what she wants. This is a very subtle distinction. She may want him to point out options and ask her questions about her needs, but she doesn't want him to make the decision or presume that she can't do it for herself.

> **A woman appreciates a dialog about her needs,
> but she doesn't want a man to
> make her decision unless she directly asks.**

On Mars, if a man sees someone he considers to be an expert, he doesn't mind at all being told what he wants. By asking questions, a man acknowledges that another has greater expertise. As a result, he wants to hear what this person thinks he should do. When women ask men a lot of questions about something, he presumes she wants him to tell her what to do.

A woman commonly experiences a man not wanting to take directions from others. This is only true when a man thinks he can do it himself. When a man is going to another for help and he perceives another person to have an expertise he doesn't, he easily accepts and appreciates direction. When a man recognizes another to be an expert, then he doesn't mind this expert presuming to know what he wants.

This dynamic is seen very clearly in medical consultations. A woman wants doctors to ask questions and answer her questions so that she can know her options and decide. A doctor who doesn't presume to know what she wants will be greatly trusted and appreciated by a woman.

Once in the doctor's office, a man basically wants to know his options, but is more interested in what the doctor thinks he should do. For a man, what a trusted doctor thinks is the bottom line. He would not be offended if the doctor said, "This is what you want to do. . . ." A man simply hears it as a plan of action or a plan of attack to solve a problem and is in no way offended.

> **Men initially resist asking for directions,**
> **but once they ask an expert they have**
> **little resistance in receiving that direction.**

In their personal relationships, men get the idea that women want men to know what women want. There is nothing more romantic than a man doing what a woman wants without her having to ask. In the workplace, this same principle holds true but in a different way. A woman in the workplace appreciates and trusts a man who gives her the service that she wants. What she doesn't want is for him to decide for her what she wants.

Another reason some women don't want a man telling her what she wants is the pressure factor. By directly telling a woman what she wants a man puts pressure on her to agree. On Venus, they have a much greater tendency to please and accommodate others. With a greater sensitivity to what others want, she can find it difficult to know what she wants. She greatly appreciates the support of a man to assist her in finding out for herself. The last thing she needs to feel is the pressure to please him by making him right when she is trying to look within herself. Instead, she would like to feel relaxed and comfortable making up her own mind.

Here are five examples of how a man might make this mistake:

1. He says, "This office on the side is exactly what you want."

Instead, he could say, "This side has a great view, would you like your office here?"

2. He says, "What you want to do is put this problem behind you and move forward. Call . . ."

Instead he could say, "Well, fortunately this problem is behind you, and you can move forward. Would you like to call . . ."

3. He says, "This is the right package for you. It gives you just what you want in a car."

Instead he could say, "This package has everything you asked for. Does it sound good to you?"

4. He says, "This location is exactly what you want. It has all the features you are looking for. You can . . ."

Instead he could say, "This is a good location. It has all the features you asked for. Would you like to look around?"

5. He says, "I could come by Thursday afternoon to show you this presentation or I am on your side of town on Friday."

Instead he could say, "Would you like me to come by to show you this presentation? I am available Thursday afternoon, and I am also on your side of town on Friday."

In each of these examples, a man presumes to know what a woman wants and makes a suggestion based on his presumption before she has decided for herself. By not asking her to make up her mind, he doesn't offend her or put pressure on her to comply with his wishes. By using this nonassuming approach, he earns her trust and increases her willingness to cooperate with him.

When a man presumes to know what a woman wants, with

the following suggestions she can assert herself in a friendly manner without feeling a pressure to please and comply:

1. He says, "This nice office on the side has a great view. It is exactly what you want."

She could say, "Why do you think so?" After he answers, she could respond, "I am not so sure, I'd like to see my other options. . . ."

2. He says, "What you want to do is put this problem behind you and move forward. Call . . ."

She could say, "I'm not so sure I am done with it. I still have some ideas that might make a difference."

3. He says, "This is the right package for you. It gives you just what you want in a car."

She could say, "Well, it's a nice package, but I still need to see more options before I am ready to buy a car."

4. He says, "This location is exactly what you want. It has all the features you are looking for. You can . . ."

She could say, "I'm glad you think so. I still need a lot more time to see what else is available, and I am not in a hurry."

5. He says, "I could come by Thursday afternoon to show you this presentation or I am on your side of town on Friday."

She could say, "Well, thank you, but I am not really ready to make a decision on this. I will get back to you soon."

By simply asserting that she has not yet decided what she wants, she is able to deflect a man's presumption without having to push him away or reject his decision. Women run the risk of alienating men by taking their presumption personally and saying, "That's not what I want."

Keep in mind that the words are not as important as the tone. Even a strong, matter-of-fact declaration, "That's not what I want," would be completely acceptable on Mars if expressed in a friendly and trusting manner. The suggested responses that appear above are particularly useful for women who have a tendency to take a man's "pushiness" personally or have difficulty standing their ground while maintaining a friendly, cooperative feeling.

10. When a Man Presumes to Understand What a Woman Is Feeling

A woman thinks a man is not listening when he presumes to understand what she is feeling. Often a man will say, "I understand," thinking he is being supportive by indicating that he is listening and knows what she is feeling. On Venus, you cannot understand until you hear it all. To say you understand can be insulting because it sounds like, "I got it already. You don't have to tell me any more. Let's move on." A Martian thinks he is listening because he thinks he understands what she is feeling. He has no idea how insulting it can be.

Women have a much greater tolerance for emotional distress. With a higher threshold, before they feel something has to be done now, they can patiently listen to another's distress without feeling an urgency to do something or fix it. A man hears a problem and wants to immediately do something about it. When she shares her feelings, he thinks she is just alerting him to the fact that there is a problem that he is supposed to solve. He doesn't realize that she wants him to listen patiently.

When he says, "I understand," he is saying he is motivated to help in some way and has heard enough to suggest a solution. What she hears is "I don't want to listen anymore. Let's either do something or change the subject."

In this example, when women think "men don't listen," it is

accurate to conclude a man listened but was incorrect in presuming to know all of what she was feeling. In addition, he assumed that she wanted a solution when she actually wanted him to hear all of her feelings before giving his point of view. Men need to remember that saying, "I understand" at the wrong time can be insulting.

Instead of saying I understand, he can assure a woman that he is listening by nodding his head and occasionally making little sounds like "umhumm," "oh," or "humph." On Venus, these kinds of reassuring gestures mean, "I am listening and trying to understand what you are saying."

> **A man can assure a woman that he is listening**
> **by making little sounds like "umhumm," "oh,"**
> **or "humph."**

A man generally doesn't nod his head or make reassuring sounds because on Mars it would mean he agrees with a woman's point of view. If she were feeling that helpless and hopeless, the last message he would want to give is that he agreed. Instead he wants to give her hope and offer his help. With this new awareness, a man can become more animated in his response to her.

11. *When a Man Presumes to Know How a Woman Should Feel*

A woman believes a man is not listening when he presumes to know how she should feel. Often a man will make comments like, "You shouldn't worry about it" or "It's not such a big deal." He believes he could not have come up with these correct assessments if he wasn't listening.

On Venus, such comments can be invalidating and are clear signs that he is not listening to her feelings with a caring heart. In this instance, when women think "men don't listen," it is accurate to conclude he listened but was incorrect in assuming that minimizing comments would be helpful. With this awareness a woman is less inclined to be offended.

On Mars, a man will often dismiss the feelings of a friend as overreactions and suggest that he not pay attention to them. A suggestion like this could put you in jail on Venus. Feelings are sacred and the validation of feelings is a way someone shows support. On Venus, minimizing feelings of distress is seen as a put-down and makes a woman feel personally attacked.

> **On Venus, feelings are sacred and the validation of feelings is a way someone shows support.**

Here are some phrases men commonly use to support one another at times of distress:

1. There's no point in complaining about it.

2. You're just overreacting.

3. It is just not a big deal.

4. Don't make it more than it is.

5. That's not what really happened.

6. It's not as bad as you think.

7. Give me a break.

8. Come on, just forget it.

9. Let's do something fun.

10. OK, I've heard enough.

11. There is no sense in beating a dead horse.

12. Can we change the subject now?

A wise man would not use these phrases with a stranger or customer. He will use them with people with whom he feels close or connected to. A wiser man will not use these phrases with a woman even if they work closely together. When a man minimizes her feelings, a woman can avoid misinterpreting his intention by realizing that he is trying to be friendly and to help.

If a woman can make light of a man's minimizing comments, she can connect more effectively with men without having to become one. When he makes a minimizing comment, she creates a sense of camaraderie and mutual respect by responding in a light manner. Here are some examples of banter to minimize stress between the sexes:

He says:	**She says to connect:**
There's no point in complaining about it.	Hey, I'm only letting off some steam.
You're just overreacting.	It's only temporary.
It is just not a big deal.	Maybe not, but let me milk it for a few more minutes.
Don't make it more than it is.	OK, OK, just hear me out, and I will be very happy.
That's not what really happened.	Let's just agree to disagree on this one.
It's not as bad as you think.	You're probably right. I'm sure I'll get over it soon.
Give me a break.	OK, but only after I finish. Just give me three more minutes to complain.
Come on, just forget it.	I know you are sick of hearing about it. I'm almost done.

He says:	She says to connect:
Let's do something fun.	You're right. There's no reason we both have to suffer. Back to work.
OK, I've heard enough.	You can handle more. Give me three more minutes and I'll really be impressed.
There is no sense in beating a dead horse.	OK, I'll stop. Let me finish, and I'll be done with it.
Can we change the subject now?	Yes, I think you have suffered enough.

This kind of playful response is not appropriate for every occasion, but in casual work situations, in private situations, or in group meetings, the playful and accepting tone will immediately discharge emotional tension that arises when men resist shared feeling.

12. A Man Changes the Subject Before She Is Finished

A woman feels a man is not listening when he changes the subject instead of asking more questions to draw her out. To a woman this is evidence that he wasn't listening. On Venus, a woman will intentionally not say everything in order for the listener to demonstrate interest by asking more questions. In pausing, she gives the other person a chance to interact. This is not only a friendly gesture, but allows the two to be more connected. When the listener asks a question, it gives the speaker a chance to clarify what she is saying according to the need of the listener. In the process of answering questions, she knows that she too will become more clear.

A woman feels heard when, after she makes a point and

pauses, the listener asks for more information. A woman concludes that if a man was listening, he would have realized that there was more to say and ask for more details.

Women demonstrate their understanding by asking more questions to express more details.

A man is often not aware of this Venusian protocol and assumes that a woman has made her point and is finished. When he doesn't ask more questions, she gets the message that he is not interested in what she has to say. In this example, when women think "men don't listen," it is accurate to conclude he listened but was incorrect in assuming that she was finished and didn't realize she wanted him to ask her more questions.

On Mars, they don't depend on others to draw them out. They get their best ideas out right away. It is important for women to realize a roundabout approach will sabotage her success in making a presentation in the workplace. A man will tend to make his most convincing points before he pauses or opens the floor for questions. He is not waiting to be drawn out with questions. When a woman does this, men assume her presentation is incomplete and filled with holes. In presenting ideas before men, a woman needs to know that she will be evaluated by her first set of ideas. It is of no value for her professional image to expect to be drawn out.

In discussions, a woman will naturally demonstrate her interest by asking questions to draw a person out. What she doesn't know is that this tendency can be offensive to men. When she asks a question, a man may get the idea that she thinks his idea was not complete. If she brings attention to something missing in his presentation, he will respect her questions. If she is attempting to demonstrate her interest by drawing him out with a few clarifying questions, she may offend him. With this insight men and women can learn to not interpret questions or the lack of questions as a personal attack.

**If a woman's questions bring attention to
something missing in his presentation,
a man will respect her questions.**

A man can avoid offending a woman by using clarifying questions instead of rushing on to make his point or give a solution. On the other hand, when a woman uses clarifying questions to draw a man out, her tactic may be offensive to him and make her look foolish, as if she didn't get it the first time. It is fine for a woman to use clarifying phrases with men as long as she is truly seeking clarification for herself and not trying to draw him out or indirectly trying to clarify his thinking for him. Here are some examples of clarifying questions:

1. So, are you saying that . . . ?

2. Do you mean that . . . ?

3. Is it really true that . . . ?

4. How can it be that . . . ?

5. You've got to be kidding, . . . ?

6. Does it make sense to say . . . ?

7. Is it most efficient to . . . ?

8. Am I to conclude that . . . ?

9. What I hear you saying is . . . is that correct?

10. What would you say if . . . ?

A woman feels supported by clarifying questions but a man may take offense. If a woman happens to feel personally attacked or challenged by what he has said, clarifying questions may seem like an attack. If a man has to defend himself, he cannot be the solution. Men get around this by not reacting personally. In many situations, they challenge each other without creating animosity by asking questions without feeling offended.

One of the things men most dread about communication in the workplace is being asked questions just for the sake of connecting. On the other hand, one of the things a man enjoys most is being the expert and being of service. If a woman asks more questions and is sure to let him know in her tone of voice how helpful his ideas and answers are, then he is happy to respond and she builds trust and respect in their work relationship.

**Men in the workplace dread being questioned
just for the sake of connecting.**

The list of clarifying questions is helpful for men to know what to say when their urge is to change the subject on a woman. These are questions a man could ask to assure her he is hearing her. This list is also helpful for women to recognize what a difference their tone of voice makes. By role-playing these questions with a mistrusting tone, a woman can get a clear sense of how she may have been pushing men away. Women can make sure men get the right message by occasionally adding upbeat comments before a question. Here are some examples:

1. This is so helpful, are you saying that . . . ?

2. That is really a good idea, do you mean that . . . ?

3. I would never have thought of that. Is it really true that . . . ?

4. This amazes me. How can it be that . . . ?

5. Who would know that? You've got to be kidding . . . ?

6. You are just the person I needed to talk to. Does it make sense to say . . . ?

7. You must be right, but is it really most efficient to . . . ?

8. This completely makes sense. Am I to conclude that . . . ?

9. This is such a good idea. Let me make sure I've got it. What I hear you saying . . . ?

10. This is great stuff. What would you say if . . . ?

By adding appreciation to her question, a man clearly gets the right idea and doesn't feel that he is being challenged. The words are not really that important, but taking the time to express a little appreciation makes a big difference.

In a similar manner, when a man takes the time to listen courteously and ask questions, his inner caring becomes more activated and is conveyed by the tone of his voice. When positive feelings are expressed in the tone of our voice, the tendency for others to take offense dramatically decreases.

A man doesn't mind being challenged as long as he senses that his words and ideas are not being taken personally. If he senses that he is being challenged from a personal perspective, it will bring out the worst in him. When men feel they are being targeted as the enemy, they respond in a defensive manner, and the attacker becomes their enemy. Men get personal when others take them personally. This is why so much in the workplace is about excluding personal feelings and sticking to the bottom line.

By becoming a bit more personal, men have the key to achieving greater success and increased harmony and cooperation with female coworkers, managers, customers, and clients. As women learn to correctly interpret male listening habits, they will minimize the tendency to sabotage their success by responding to male behavior in a personal manner. With this increased understanding and respect in the workplace everyone wins.

8

Rules Are from Mars, Manners Are from Venus

Men tend to follow a set of unspoken rules to minimize giving offense in the competitive and impersonal work environment. By following these rules, a man's workplace behavior and actions affirm that his decisions and motivations are not personal. You may like someone or be a friend, but decision making is primarily based on what is required to achieve the bottom line.

Women tend to follow a set of manners and customs that are nurturing and relationship-oriented. Though this approach is particularly useful in raising children, it is also useful in the workplace to create harmony, cooperation, collaboration, alliances, and loyalty. When a customer or client is faced with a choice, and all things are equal, they will always follow their sense of loyalty and connection. Personal connections can be the deciding factor to close a deal.

**Personal connections can be the deciding factor
to close a deal.**

The new workplace has dramatically changed. The old rules from Mars were particularly effective in an environment of limited communication and choice, but today they are outdated. Unless men begin to break the old rules, they will find themselves lagging behind. With new technological advances in the speed and effectiveness of communication, employees and consumers have more choice. Staying competitive in this changing world market requires a balance of Martian and Venusian rules, manners, and values.

**Unless men begin to break the old rules, they will find
themselves lagging behind their competition.**

The old rules from Mars are often in direct opposition to the relationship-oriented manners and customs from Venus. Acceptable and respectable behavior on Mars often makes women feel excluded betrayed, and unable to trust. On the other hand, nurturing Venusian manners and customs can often be seen as signs of weakness on Mars. By understanding Martian rules, a woman gains the edge for getting ahead in the many areas of the workplace that are male dominated.

To develop a new style of doing business, it is essential for both men and women in the workplace to recognize how they may be violating the rules and manners from their different worlds. With a growing awareness of how we can be more supportive of each other, the workplace can and will reflect a more harmonious blend of Martian rules and Venusian manners.

It is a big adjustment for many women to shift to a Martian competitive environment in which the most pragmatic solution to achieve greater income and productivity is the goal. This challenge becomes even greater when a woman doesn't understand the workplace rules from Mars.

These rules are not secret, but they are unspoken. Women are not purposely excluded from this important information. For men, they are part instinct and part learned from playing competitive sports. Unless a woman grew up with lots of brothers, it is very difficult for her to decipher these rules.

Some women "get it" automatically because they are simply born with higher levels of Martian hormones. Instinctively they relate to the same set of rules as men. These women are often the ones who get ahead in business. But for most women, they need to learn the rules men are following to experience greater success.

Women with higher levels of Martian hormones relate better with men and as a result get ahead in business.

Imagine trying to play basketball without knowing the rules. You would feel confused and mistreated all the time. You would unknowingly be causing fouls and calling fouls. You wouldn't know why you were losing. Without understanding the different plays and strategies, you would be a detriment to your team.

No matter how talented you are or how hard you try, if you don't know the rules you don't succeed.

Without an understanding of the guiding rules for men in the workplace, men may appear to women as arrogant, insensitive, demanding, and uncaring when they are just doing their job and respecting the rules from Mars that govern a competitive workplace. In their personal relationships, these same men could be kind, generous, considerate, and forgiving. Even in their work relationships these characteristics may be present, but to someone who doesn't understand their rules they just don't appear that way.

Creating Change in the Workplace

Success in any arena in life increases when we respect the old and make room for the new. This kind of synthesis of opposite values is the secret of creativity and progress.

**A synthesis of Martian and Venusian values is
the secret of creativity and progress.**

The old Martian rules need to be updated. This process, however, takes time. In the meantime, if you know the rules by which others are playing you can choose how you want to play. At least when others call foul you will know why. When others don't want you on their team, you will not take it personally but recognize that you are the one who is unwilling to play by their rules. When others seek to tackle or bring you down, you will not take it personally.

In a seminar I was teaching in London, I referred to my own experience of this with the news media. I explained, "Occasionally, an interviewer will appear to be very friendly and then turn around and say some of the nastiest and mean-spirited things in an article or report. Practically anything you say, when taken out of context, can be fashioned to make whatever point the interviewer wants to make. When the intent is to do an 'axe job,' they can make anyone appear however they wish."

After I mentioned this, a woman stood up and announced that she was one of those reporters. Her simple statement was, "Try to be forgiving. If we don't sound cynical and tough, our publishers will not print our articles and then we don't get paid. If you look deeper, we are also saying some of the good things you say as well."

This completely changed my perspective. For the most part

she was right. I shouldn't take it so personally. They were just following their set of rules and doing what their job required. When I stopped taking it personally, my public life became much more relaxed. Instead of focusing on the negative, I could also see the positive.

The work world is sometimes unfair, cold, manipulative, and corrupt. But it can be supportive, respectful, enriching, and fulfilling. It is an imperfect system created by imperfect people. To expect perfection is setting yourself up to be disappointed. Gradually the workplace is improving.

You can play by the rules or not. The choice is yours. If you want to change the rules you first have to respect the rules. The only way to change the rules is to work with them. Taking them personally only alienates you and limits your power to make a positive change.

Ultimately, Martian rules and Venusian manners are not better than the other. They are just different. They each have a context in which they are most appropriate. When the context changes, then the rules need to change as well. When men and women work side by side, the context changes. Those who are able to adjust through respecting others as well as themselves are the ones who rise to the top.

> **Those who are able to adjust through respecting others as well as themselves are the ones who rise to the top.**

By respecting and appreciating Martian rules and Venusian manners, a synthesis can be achieved and a new and better set of rules and customs will develop.

Business and Competitive Sports

On Mars, the rules of business are sometimes like the rules of competitive sports. In the ring and on the courts and fields of competition, they literally fight each other. Their main objective is to beat their opponent and win. As long as certain rules are followed, then everything else is fair, and no one takes the competition personally. The objective is to do your best and may the best man win.

After the game, they may be the best of friends, but during the game their objective is to beat the other. They do their very best to win. Part of that process is strategizing and planning how to defeat their opponent. They are always concerned with the score and feel happiest when they are winning.

In sports like archery, bowling, and golf you can compete with yourself to do your best, but in other sports like tennis, basketball, football, baseball, and boxing you are more actively competing with others. The rules of Mars particularly apply to these more competitive sports. The bottom line, although it may seem heartless on Venus, is that you want them to lose so that you can win.

You do your best to wear them down, strike them out, tackle them, or even knock them out. To do anything less would be an insult. No Martian wants to feel as if the opposing team or opponent "let them win." A sporting event is a test of skill and talent. For someone to win, then someone must loose.

These more competitive sports reflect the rules from Mars. These rules allow men to engage in this kind of warfare without taking it personally. They can seek to beat their opponent without actually wanting to hurt each other. They "mean" to win, but they are not cruel. They want to win fair and square. They want to win at all costs, but they follow the rules and don't purposefully kick below the waist. By following agreed-upon rules,

they gain honor while defeating a foe. If the rules are not followed, then even if they win they lose honor.

**Rules in sports allow men to engage in a kind of warfare
without taking it personally.**

This is different from the thinking on Venus. There they play
by different rules. They want others to win and not themselves.
Sacrifice and unconditional giving are highly revered. As long as
everyone has this attitude, then everyone is taken care of.

On Venus, when everyone gives, then everyone gets.

This giving approach works on Venus but not in sports and
not in a Martian work world. You cannot win a basketball game
if you keep giving the ball to the opponent or by setting them up
to make a winning shot. You do your best to keep the ball and
block their shots. This direct opposition is friendly and fair, because everyone has the same opportunity. In this way, the best
and most skilled team wins.

In a work world populated by Venusians, if a man seeks to
win the trust and respect of women, he needs to understand the
customs and manners from Venus. For example, in the Venusian
world of business, sometimes the way to win clients is to refer
them to someone else more qualified for their needs. They will
remember that you cared about them and as a result support you
more.

With the influx of women in the work world, the old rules
are gradually changing. The old "I win, you lose mentality" is
sometimes being replaced where appropriate with a new and improved "I win and you win." Certainly companies still seek to
beat their competition, but between coworkers, between management and coworkers, and between service providers and

clients, this win/win attitude is taking over. Win/Win is a synthesis of Martian and Venusian thinking. By taking the time to respect and honor differences in the workplace, you will be creating the fertile ground for both men and women to experience equal opportunities for increasing success.

Mars and Venus in the Boardroom

When men sit at a board meeting, they may become involved in heated debates, but no one takes it personally. They may get angry, become frustrated, disappointed, or express worry. It is not intended to be taken personally, nor is it taken personally.

At noon, when it's time for lunch, men will go off together and have a good time at lunch. They will go out of their way to make sure that the message is clear, business is business and nothing is to be taken personally. By having a good time together or sharing a drink, they reinforce the message that there are no hard feelings.

> **Men go out of their way to reinforce the message that there are no hard feelings.**

It is quite different when a group of women from various departments get together and argue. In the work world, a woman has to sell an idea. If the idea isn't accepted, often a woman doesn't feel heard or respected, and as a result stress increases.

When it's time for lunch, instead of going off together like men, women will purposely go off in different directions to discuss more intimately with a friend or coworker what was said. In this way, she gets to release her tension and stress by feeling heard.

On Venus, when women share in their support groups, the dynamic is different from women sharing in the workplace. Each woman feels heard and validated. This is much easier to do when you do not have to make business decisions, changes, and evaluations, or when one person is the boss and makes the final decision.

This kind of stress for women is dramatically increased when men and women meet together in challenging meetings. Men unknowingly express themselves in ways that make women feel personally attacked. At such times a woman may respond in ways that express anger, resentment, frustration, hurt, disappointment, worry, fear, and mistrust. As we have already explored, this only antagonizes men. Immediately a woman's case loses its merit in the eyes of men, simply by the way she presents it.

Equality in the Workplace

When people seek equality in the workplace, they generally want more pay, more opportunities, and more privileges. We see others getting more, and we want it. Without a clear understanding of how the workplace operates, resentment begins to build.

With this new understanding of how men and women think, feel, and communicate differently in the workplace, we share an equal opportunity to earn the respect of others in the workplace. Even though this equality of opportunity is available, there is no such thing as equality in the workplace.

Everyone gets different pay and privileges and always will. In a free economy, we compete to get more, it is not just given to us. Our pay or worth is regulated by supply and demand. If your service is in demand and the supply is low, your value goes up. As a result, you get more respect. For example, if you are the only person who can fix the computer, when you arrive there is great reverence and wonder in the air. If the office is filled with programmers with similar ability, your talent is not even noticed.

In a free economy there are no free rides.
We have to earn our way.

As a woman learns the rules that govern how men think, she can make a few small adjustments and earn his respect just as any other man would have to earn his respect. This can also be done without having to become a Martian. It is not that men don't respect women. Men don't respect certain behaviors that violate the unspoken rules from Mars. When anyone, man or woman, violates these rules for business and professionalism then he or she loses the respect of men.

To gain respect in the workplace it must be earned.

This may seem unfair, because women have to behave and communicate in ways determined by men for men to respect them. But men face the same adjustment. If men want to enlist the respect and support of women, they have to change the way they behave and interact.

Understanding the rules from Mars will also assist some men who are not getting the respect they deserve from men. If a man grew up in a family of girls, was very close to his mother, didn't play team sports, or just has lower levels of Martian hormones, sometimes he also doesn't relate to these rules.

In a similar manner, women who grew up with brothers, played competitive sports, were closer to their father, or were born with higher levels of Martian hormones will instinctively relate more to rules from Mars.

Comparing Martian Rules and Venusian Manners

Let's summarize these rules from Mars and compare them to complementary manners from Venus. Remember: one is not better than the other. The point of looking at these differences is to understand how you may be misinterpreting others or how others may be misinterpreting you.

Rules from Mars:

Talk about a problem only if you have a solution.

Using the least number of words to make a point demonstrates competence.

Don't put yourself down. It weakens your power to lead.

Showing feelings is a sign of weakness, and your enemies will use it against you.

Always have an answer and never reveal the feeling of uncertainty.

Show strength and confidence by not taking offense.

Contain feelings: stay cool, collected, and calm and others will respect you more.

Only ask for help if you really need it. You are evaluated and respected by what you do on your own.

It is up to you to close every deal or get what you want. If you don't ask, you won't get.

Manners from Venus:

When there is a problem, talk about it.

Sharing details of your experiences develops rapport and strengthens work relationships.

Don't build yourself up above others. It creates division.

Share vulnerable feelings to build trust and get support.

Don't assume you have the best answer. Include others in the problem-solving process.

Demonstrate caring and self-worth by taking offense at disrespect.

Express personal feelings to increase mutual understanding and support.

Giving and receiving helps generate a sense of connection, collaboration, and team spirit.

Demonstrate your commitment by doing your very best, and others will automatically notice and reward you.

Rules from Mars:

The rule of efficiency: Never do what you don't have to do. If you do more, make sure you are compensated.

Always take credit for what you do, and let it be known. Promote yourself, and others will promote you.

Business is business: Let the bottom line determine your decisions and not sentiment.

The end justifies the means: measure success by the end result and not the process.

Manners from Venus:

The golden rule: Do unto others as you would have them do unto you. Give more and you will get more.

Always give credit to those who have helped you. Promote others, and they will promote you.

You scratch my back and I will scratch yours. Remember your friends, and they will remember you.

Success is a journey and not a destination. It's not what you do, but how you do it.

With this increased awareness you can adjust your behavior and responses according to the context in which you are working. If you are working with a woman or a group of women, then you would want to brush up on your Venusian manners. If you are working with a man or a group of men, then it's helpful to remind yourself of how you may be evaluated.

By taking these rules and manners into consideration, you will be better prepared to choose your responses and interact in a manner that is most appropiate.

How to Ask for Support and Get It

When you are not getting the support you want in the workplace, a significant reason may be that you do not ask enough or you ask in a way that doesn't work. When it comes to asking for support, the rules and manners on Mars and Venus are completely different. Men often have a greater resistance to asking for directions but more easily ask for increased compensation. To ask for directions implies not being able to do something, but to ask for compensation implies getting what you deserve because you are able to do something. Women tend to ask for both support and compensation, but in ways that are easily overlooked or are misinterpreted on Mars.

A woman often asks for support in ways that are too indirect for men to even realize that she is asking. On the other hand, a man will tend to be too blunt or sound disrespectful. By taking into consideration how our requests are heard by the opposite sex we can be much more successful in getting the respect we deserve, the support we need, and the cooperation we want.

Why Women Don't Ask

Women often make the mistake of thinking that they don't have to directly ask for support. Because on Venus they intuitively feel the needs of others and give whatever they can, they mistakenly expect men in the workplace to do the same. When women work together they are always checking to see if their help is needed. A woman by instinct looks with great delight and enthusiasm for ways to offer her support. The more she respects, appreciates, or cares about someone the more she will offer her support and not wait to be asked. Back on Venus, everyone automatically gives support, so there is no reason to ask for it. When men in the workplace don't notice her needs or readily offer their support, a woman mistakenly concludes that she is not respected or appreciated.

**A woman loses support by not asking, but a man loses
points by not offering her support.**

Women tend to indirectly ask for support in two ways: by
giving a lot or by expressing negative feelings about a problem.
On Mars it is not enough to just give support and expect it to
come back. When a woman happily gives her support but doesn't
directly ask for support or compensation in return, a man concludes that she is already getting what she needs. In the second
case, if she expresses feelings of frustration or worry while
talking about a problem, unless she directly asks for him to assist her he may not offer. He may give her a suggestion but he
will not do something.

A man withholds his active support not because he is unwilling to help. He is just "respectfully" waiting to be asked. Remember that on Mars they don't offer unsolicited help or assistance. If she doesn't directly ask, then he mistakenly concludes
that she wants to do it herself. To motivate a man, a woman
needs to develop the art of directly asking for support. This is
helpful not just in getting support but also in getting raises, more
staff and increased benefits and job perks. Unless a woman does-
n't directly ask, a man will not offer to give his support.

**When a woman happily gives her support, a man
concludes that she is already getting what she needs.**

When a woman doesn't directly ask for what she wants, a
man concludes that she doesn't want it or that she is already getting what she wants and needs. A man might even quietly wonder why a woman doesn't ask for his assistance while she is
struggling with a problem. At the same time the woman is wondering or resenting why he hasn't offered his assistance. When
she doesn't ask he mistakenly concludes that she wants to do it
herself or that she is already getting enough support.

**When a woman doesn't ask, a man concludes that she is
already getting what she wants or needs.**

A wise man scores a lot of points by going overboard to notice when she might need assistance and support. Often when he
offers his unsolicited support, even if she doesn't want his support he will get points for offering. This is when it is important
for men to remember that it is the little things that count on
Venus. By making small gestures of support a man is assured of
winning a woman's support and creating a mutually supportive
work environment.

Earning Admiration on Venus

Ultimately the way for a man to get ahead in the workplace
today is to earn the respect and admiration of women coworkers, managers, employees, clients, and consumers. There is nothing that earns admiration faster than offering to give support in
little ways. It is not enough to be completely willing to do what
she asks. It is not enough to say, "All you had to do is ask and I
would have been happy to help." Instead, he gets the most points
by noticing how he may be needed and offering his support.

Often a man will think he is offering his support but a
woman hears criticism. He will ask a question instead of directly
offering his support. He may be thinking, "Maybe she needs
help sorting those new forms. If she hasn't done it yet I will do it
for her."

Instead of directly offering to help he will mistakenly say something like, "Did you finish sorting the new forms?" He doesn't
want to offer his support unless he knows she really needs it. This
tendency comes from Mars. On his planet he may insult another
by offering help unless it is clearly needed. To simply offer help implies that another Martian can't handle what he is doing.

Asking if a woman has finished sorting the new forms may completely backfire. If she is already feeling a little stressed and she hasn't yet done the forms, his question may sound like he is pushing her to do more when she is already doing as much as she can. She might react by telling him to mind his own business or resent him for meddling.

What would work instead is to directly offer his support without asking first if it is needed. He should just say, "May I help sort out these forms for you?" Or he could just take charge in a friendly way and say, "Where are those new forms that need to be sorted? I have some extra time. Let me sort them out." By using "May I" or "Let me" a man is asking permission to give rather than putting a woman in the position of having to directly ask for support.

> **By using "May I" or "Let me" a man makes it easier
> for a woman to accept his support.**

By asserting himself in this supportive manner he will earn big points with her. Another way to earn her admiration and support is to avoid asking if she would *like* him to do something for her. He needs to remember that if she is not directly asking him, then she is probably waiting for him to offer his support if he is willing. Asking if she would "like" his support is not the same as offering his support. It is just a question, which then puts the responsibility back on her to ask. If she is already uncomfortable asking, then she will probably say "No, it's OK. Thanks anyway."

> **Asking if she would "like" his support is not
> the same as offering his support.**

Instead of saying, "Would you *like* my help?" he should say, "May I help you?" By this small change she will be much more willing to accept his help and he will earn her admiration. When men say, "Would you like my help?" or "Can I help?" women will often say no when they really mean yes. On her planet she is really saying, "Well, I don't want to be demanding, but if you have the extra time I would really appreciate the help. Just insist on helping and I will accept your help."

> **When men say, "Would you like my help?" or**
> **"Can I help?" women will often say no**
> **when they really mean yes.**

When a woman wants to help she will instinctively just join in and start helping. On Venus, they are collaborators. In a co-operative environment, help is always welcome. A Venusian would not offer to help by saying, "Would you like my help?" Unless they were saying something like, "If you really need my help then I will help. Otherwise I have other things to do."

To summarize these points of offering support, here is a list of what to say, what not to say, and an interpretation of what she may hear if a man offers his support without being direct.

How to Offer Women Unsolicited Support

Direct offering for support. Do say:	Indirect offering of support. Don't say:	What she may hear when a man is not direct:
Let me help you with that.	Would you like my help sorting out these new forms?	I will help if you really need it but I have other more pressing things to do.
This has been such a busy day. Let me help you sort those papers.	Do you need help?	I am already doing a lot but if you really need help again then I will help.

Direct offering for support. Do say:	Indirect offering of support. Don't say:	What she may hear when a man is not direct:
I have some extra time. May I help by sorting these papers?	What can I do to help?	You are quite scattered today. If you really need help I can help.
Let me help you finish sorting those papers.	Are you finished sorting those papers?	You should have finished those papers by now.
May I suggest that you do this tomorrow? We don't need those forms right away.	Why don't you do that tomorrow?	You are not very good at prioritizing. Maybe tomorrow you will get it right.
This has been a really busy day. Let me ask Tom to help sort out these new forms.	Did you ask Tom to help you sort these forms?	You are not very good at collaborating and getting the help of others.
You have all those calls to make. Let me help sort out these new forms.	Why don't you finish your calls and I will sort out these papers?	You can't seem to figure out what to do here so I will give you some directions.
I have some extra time. Let me finish sorting those papers.	Will you have time to finish sorting those papers?	You are taking too much time.

Why Women Become Resentful

Women are often uncomfortable asking for more. They do not want to risk offending a person by asking for too much. A woman may "hint around" but not directly ask for what she wants. As a result she postpones directly asking until she feels resentful. Then, motivated by a sense of injustice, she will leave her comfort zone and make demands. By asking in a tone of resentment, suddenly her achievements shrink in a man's eyes and his willingness to reward her decreases.

To earn respect in the workplace women need to recognize the importance of directly asking and adjusting the way they think they are asking. On Mars, if you don't clearly ask, you don't get. To get more or get ahead you have to ask and then ask again. But it is not as simple as that. *How* you ask as well as how *much* you ask for have a big impact on what you get.

Five Tips for Direct Asking

There are five secrets for asking for support on Mars and receiving it. Most men will not necessarily be aware of these secrets but they will instinctively follow them. They are appropriate timing, nondemanding attitude, being brief, being direct, and using correct wording. Let's explore each more closely:

1. Appropriate timing: Be careful not to ask him to do something that he is obviously just planning to do. For example, if he is rushing to finish a report, it can be insulting to say, "Could you finish that report for me today?" He may feel controlled and unappreciated for his efforts. Instead, if she is wanting to be assured that he will finish, then she should be direct about her question. She could say, "Do you think you will be done today?"

Timing is very important even when a woman does apply the other secrets of direct asking. When a man is focused on another task he will experience a lot of resistance to her requests if she interrupts him. This resistance is not to her request but to the interruption. It is not that he is unwilling to do what she has asked but that he is resisting having to stop doing what he is doing to consider her request. Whenever a woman can wait for him to take a break or shift his focus, that is the best time to ask.

If she has to interrupt she can still be successful by simply acknowledging that she is interrupting with an "excuse me." In this situation she needs to be careful to simply make her request and not take it personally when he grumbles about it. By her overlooking his resistance this time, he will be more willing to support in the future. If, however, at a later time he concludes that her interruption wasn't necessary or reasonable, then his respect for her will go down.

When in doubt she can also just ask if this is a good time to talk about a pressing issue. This gives him control and he will feel less interrupted. He may then ask, What is it? This puts the responsibility back on him to decide and he will be less resistant and respect her more. By her respecting his "cave time" he can then decide when he wants to respond.

2. Nondemanding Attitude: A request is not a demand. Men don't respond well to demands or ultimatums. A woman doesn't like demands either, but she will respect a demand if it is backed by valid reasons, feelings, and justifications. This is a big difference between men and women. When a man is approached and someone demands his time, attention, or resources he will immediately take offense. Because he feels he is being controlled instead of hearing the validity of a request, he will begin defending his right not to do it.

When men are dealing with female clients, coworkers, managers and employees, they need to recognize that when a woman makes a demand she needs to be heard without his defenses. In this way a man can score points with her. On the other hand, if a woman is seeking to most successfully get what she wants, then she needs to focus on how to ask in a manner that is more accepting and appreciative and not angry, resentful, or demanding.

A woman will often bend over backward making sacrifices

for others, and when she doesn't get the service or support that she feels she deserves, she will take it personally and react emotionally and sound demanding. This will only make a man more defensive, and she is more likely to get more resistance rather than friendly and sincere support. Let's explore an example:

Carol had finally finished her Web site and needed to set up a new Internet service provider. As she was installing it, she ran into a number of problems. She called customer service and was treated with very little patience and understanding, and received no help. She felt the urge to get angry with the man she talked to. She felt the urge to let him know how she felt but instead decided to hold back and just get off the line. She felt defeated and helpless.

Then she decided to try the Mars-Venus approach of direct asking. Already she had taken the first important step. She didn't get angry at the man. She took a little time to cool off and then called him back to practice being direct in a nondemanding manner.

She realized that to ask for support in a nondemanding manner she had to first give some support. She first found something to compliment him for. She told him she really appreciated him talking to her in the previous call. Then, in a friendly way, she told him she was still stuck. She said, "I don't know if you can help with this one—I'm not really good with computers."

This appealed to a man's ever-present desire to be trusted, accepted, and appreciated. She was amazed that this time he became incredibly helpful and was even hard to get off the phone. In the end he said, "Don't hesitate to call back if you have any other problems; and if I'm not here, ask for Eric." He was motivated by feeling needed, by having a problem to solve, by being appreciated, and by having his style accepted.

Instead of taking it personally that in her first call he was not so helpful, she called back and instead of feeling justified to make a demand she did the opposite and made peace by asking for his support in a nondemanding manner.

3. Being brief: When asking for support or for a raise, avoid giving a list of reasons why he should help. The more you feel as if you have to convince him the weaker your position becomes in his eyes. Being brief demonstrates confidence and a sense of worthiness for what you are asking. If you feel the need to explain yourself, then it is sign you think he may not want to support you. This is not as appealing or motivating to a man as coming from a more confident position that assumes and trusts he will want to give you the support you are asking for.

Long explanations validating your request may make him feel as though you don't trust him to support you. He may feel that you are trying to convince him to be supportive when he is already willing to be supportive. Ironically, by trying to convince him he will become less willing to be supportive. A man doesn't want to hear a long list of reasons or explanations about why he should fulfill a request.

A woman will give a list of reasons to justify her needs because she has mistakenly concluded that he doesn't really want to support her, otherwise he would have already offered her his support. With this insight, which explains why men don't offer their support, a woman can correctly interpret that a man would be willing to support but he just needs the green light with a brief request. After making a brief request, if he needs a reason, then he will ask for it, and then she can give some reasons. Even then they should be cautiously brief.

4. Being direct: Women often think they are asking for men's support when on Mars they are not. When a woman wants assistance or support she may present the problem but not directly ask. A direct request does not *imply* a request. By clearly focusing on what she wants and spelling it out very clearly in the fewest words she will get the most support. Occasionally an indirect request is fine, but if she is not getting the support she wants, then by being more direct she will experience immediate results.

When a woman doesn't express herself in a direct manner it leaves room for a man to hear all kinds of messages that sound like she is demanding, criticizing, disapproving, or blaming. These kinds of messages don't generate in him a feeling of cooperation or a willingness to support her.

What He May Hear When She Is Nondirect

Brief and direct. What she should say:	Avoid being indirect. What she should not say:	What he may hear when she is indirect:
Would you handle this order?	I have to pick up the tickets and I don't have time to handle this order.	You should pick them up, otherwise you are not very supportive. (demand)
Would you copy these papers and send them out by five?	These papers still need to be copied and sent out by five.	You are supposed to do this. I should not have to be asking you again. (expectation)
Would you check out what happened to the package?	That package has still not arrived.	You haven't been on top of this delivery. You should be more responsible. (criticism)
Would your department take care of making this change?	Your department is responsible for making this change.	It is your fault that this didn't happen. (blame)
Would you take charge of handling this? I need it ASAP.	This has not worked out at all.	I am not pleased with your work. (dissatisfaction)

Brief and direct. What she should say:	Avoid being indirect. What she should not say:	What he may hear when she is indirect:
Would you clean up this mess. I don't know what to do.	This is a big mess. I really don't know what to do.	You didn't organize this properly. You should be more responsible. (rejection)
Would you pick this up around three? I am still working on it.	I should have finished by now but I still have more work to do. I don't think I can be done by twelve.	You should do this because there is no other solution. If you don't then you are not very considerate. (obligation)
Would you replace the printer paper when you use it up?	You used up all the printer paper again.	You forgot to replace the printer paper again. You don't listen to me. (disapproval)
Would you schedule some time so that we can talk about this? How about today at four?	We still haven't talked about this.	You are not respecting my needs. You should be more supportive. (resentment)

5. Using Correct Wording: When it comes to asking, men are very particular. One of the most common mistakes in asking for support is the use of "could" and "can" in place of "would" and "will." "Could you handle this problem?" is merely a question gathering information. "Would you handle this problem?" is a direct request.

Women often use "Could you" to imply "Would you." On her planet it seems more polite to indirectly ask "Could you do it?" When used occasionally, indirect requests may go unnoticed, but persistently using them may begin to irritate men. They may not even know why, but they just don't like it. In most cases a man will tend to forget her request if it is not direct.

The Magic of Using "Would" Instead of "Could"

In my seminars I have trained thousands of women in this art of direct asking and they repeatedly have had immediate success. By just asking in a way that men can understand clearly, women suddenly get a completely different response from men.

Here is one of thousands of success stories. In one company, Kelly, a receptionist, found the male sales reps who worked for the company to be a constant source of frustration. She wanted to leave work right at 5:00 P.M. because she had a child in childcare. She would ask all the sales reps to bring down their typing for her to do prior to 4:00 P.M. This would give her time to type them up and make sure she got them back by the end of the day. That way she could leave work on time. Although she asked again and again, the sales reps would inevitably always forget and not do it.

After learning how to ask in a more direct manner that works on Mars, she immediately got a different result. As most women do, she would use the phrase "Could you" instead of "Would you." "Could you" is indirect while "Would you" is direct. Men are very literal about his. If you say, "Could you . . ." he will automatically say without thinking, "Well, sure, I can do that." Using "Could you" literally means "Do you have the ability?" What man is going to say, "No, I don't have the ability to bring these papers to you"?

> To a man, "Could you" sounds like
> a question and not a request.

One of the problems with using "Could you" is that men answer the question without thinking much. However, if you ask "Would you . . ." then he has to think. Then a different part of his brain responds and says, "Hmm, let me think, am I willing to do that? Why should I do it? What would happen if I didn't do it? What will I have to do in order to do that and am able to do it?"

When a woman uses "Would you" a man doesn't automatically respond with a yes. Instead he will consider it for a few moments. By thinking more about her request he will tend to remember it more and feel a greater commitment to getting it done.

When a man says yes to a "Would you" request he feels as if he is making a promise. If he says yes to a "Could you" request then he is simply answering a question. At the time he may be fully aware of her request and even be willing to do what she has asked but still forget to do it.

When a man says yes to a "Would you" request he feels as if he is making a promise.

Kelly learned that men often forget when a woman uses "Could you" instead of "Would you." Instead of "Could you" she used the phrase "Would you." By that one simple change, there was an instant result.

Because the sales reps had to actually stop and think about "would" they or "wouldn't" they bring it down by 4:00 P.M., in most cases they started bringing it down because they had made that conscious choice.

The difference between "Would you" and "Could you" made a huge difference, and eventually she had a ninety-eight percent strike rate with them always bringing their typing to her before 4:00 P.M. Using "would" not only made her job easier but it released the huge tension that had built up between the administrative staff and the sales department.

9

Setting Boundaries

In the workplace, setting boundaries is an essential requirement for earning respect. How you communicate your boundaries determines the degree of respect that you get. Others cannot respect your boundaries unless you make them known in a manner that can be understood. It is naïve to expect others to anticipate all our wants, needs and wishes, particularly when they may have a completely different set of values and sensitivities. To achieve greater success it is essential that we both say no to what we don't want and directly ask for what we do want.

Others cannot respect your boundaries unless you make them known.

Men and women set boundaries or say "no" in different ways. Often a man doesn't hear a woman's "no" and persists in a behavior she does not accept or appreciate. Although her way of setting boundaries would be clearly recognized on her planet, he doesn't get her message. On the other hand, a woman will hear "no" when a man is actually willing to be supportive. Women often perceive boundaries where they don't exist and feel excluded.

To experience greater trust and respect in the workplace it is essential that men and women develop greater sensitivity to what is really being said. To successfully respect a woman, a man needs to clearly recognize when a woman sets a boundary. Otherwise he oversteps his boundaries and loses her trust and limits her willingness to cooperate and work together. By respecting her boundaries a man can automatically earn her trust and respect.

> **To successfully respect a woman, a man needs to clearly recognize when a woman sets a boundary.**

In a similar way, women need to recognize how they may be easily overlooked and learn ways to assert themselves so that a man will clearly get her message. This feat is not instinctive to a woman. She may think she is making herself clear, but a man will not get the message she wants to give. With greater insight into how men and women differently approach setting boundaries and asking for what we want, we can both become more successful in giving and receiving support in the workplace.

Setting Boundaries on Venus and Mars

On Venus, they are less competitive and more cooperative than on Mars. Setting limits is not as important when others are primarily collaborating with you and you are all sharing the credit equally. Standing up for yourself and standing out is not so important when no one is trying to take what you have. It is even considered bad manners. When the cultural emphasis is on sharing, the slightest indication of a boundary is immediately noticed and respected.

Because of her increased sensitivity to boundaries, a woman concludes that a man is saying no when he may be saying "yes," "maybe," "later," or "not right now." Sensing his resistance, a woman will not ask for support or persist in asking for support, because she hears a firm no. What sounds like a firm no is not so firm on Mars.

Men express boundaries differently, because on Mars they are primarily competitive. They are always fighting battles to prove themselves and claim new territories of success. Even within a company, they are competing with each other to stand up higher and stand out as more competent in some manner. In this environment, you have to put a lot more attention on making your boundaries bold, clear, definite, and distinct.

When a woman is hesitant or subtle in setting a limit, a man interprets that to mean that it is not a definite boundary, or she is unsure. If he concludes that she is indefinite, then naturally he will continue to persist. She thinks she is giving him clear signals, but to him they are too subtle to detect. When she gets annoyed, he feels unfairly judged or rejected. By understanding the way women think and feel, a man can be more aware of her subtle messages, and a woman can learn to *appear* more decisive.

Why Men Get Pushy

On Venus everyone is cared for, but on Mars, if you don't produce, you don't eat. Men are much more motivated to take whatever they can get. With everyone trying to take your job or your market share, men become much more defensive and protective of what is theirs. Unless they get a clear message that they are not welcome, they will often persist in order to get what they want.

On Venus they will go to great lengths to comfort or support a person from feeling excluded. On Mars, they will go to great lengths to be included at the next level up on the ladder of success. While a woman waits to be included, a man will assert himself. A woman senses if she is not invited that she is not welcome. A man assumes that if he is not invited he has not yet earned his way in.

**A man assumes that if he is not included
he has to earn his way in.**

As a result, men see "limits" not as stop signs but as challenges to overcome. This tendency frees a man to avoid taking rejection personally, but it makes him prone to stepping on a woman's feet. On Mars, he learns that if he wants to set a clear limit he has to be very blunt with other Martians. Unless he is very clear, he will be challenged again and again. When a woman seems the slightest bit uncertain, a man interprets that as a sign that she is still open to being persuaded or sold on something.

On Mars, if a man hears no, it doesn't mean no. He will hear "later," "not yet," or "tell me more." If a Martian really means no, he will make it very clear and blunt, because he understands that a man will often keep persisting. This tendency is reflected in sports. In baseball a man gets three strikes before he is out. If he misses the ball he always gets two more tries. He can even hit a few foul balls and not be penalized.

**On Mars, if a man hears no, he will hear "later,"
"not yet," or "tell me more."**

Though this attitude is instinctively understood by men and reinforced through competitive sports, it is not immediately apparent to a woman. On her planet, a simple look of disapproval or hesitancy is often enough to say "stop" and another woman will stop. When she says, "I don't think I am interested in this," a man interprets her hesitancy as permission to persist. On her planet she is just being polite while also setting a limit.

Assertive Communication

To assert oneself is to express a message with confidence. The best assertiveness technique for setting a boundary is repetition. Repeating a boundary is even more powerful if it is done without any expression of emotion. By expressing annoyance or anger, a woman will only make a man defensive. By setting a boundary in a neutral tone and repeating it, a woman allows a man to save face. A nonemotional response meets his need for feeling accepted at a time when he may feel rejected.

When she says in a nonemotional tone, "I am definitely not interested," a man can hear no without feeling personally rejected. If, however, she gets annoyed or angry and says the same thing, he may take offense. When she can stay strong *and* nonemotional, a man will not get defensive. If she has to repeat her request three times, she needs to take a stronger stance and say, "I have told you three times. I want you to respect my wishes." This is a more respectful way of saying, "What is it about no that you don't understand?" When setting a boundary, it is not up to a woman to comfort a man, this just makes it seem as if her boundary is not definite. When setting a boundary, a man needs her neutral clarity and not her assurance.

> **If she has to repeat her request three times, she needs to take a stronger stance to set a limit.**

These are some common ways women set subtle limits, and examples of how she could be more definite. Column one contains examples of indefinite boundaries that would work on Venus but not on Mars. In column two are examples of more definite boundaries. If a man continues to push after a woman sets her boundary, she can listen briefly and then clearly respond by repeating the same phrase. If a person is very pushy and she has to repeat a definite boundary, then she needs to move on to the stronger boundaries listed in the third column. These stronger boundaries may seem rude but they are not. On Mars, if a person is being pushy, it is an appropriate response.

Indefinite boundary:	Definite boundary:	Stronger boundary:
Maybe you could come another time.	Right now I cannot talk with you. You may call back next Thursday to make an appointment.	I have told you three times: Call back next Thursday.
We might already have too many people.	We already have too many people. There is no room for you.	I have told you three times. I want you to respect my request and leave.
This might not be the best time.	This is not a good time. Call me next week.	I have told you three times: Call me next week.
I'm not sure if I want to buy this.	I will need more time to consider this purchase. I will call you in a few weeks and let you know.	I have told you three times: I will let you know in a few weeks.
I don't think this is exactly what we are looking for.	This is not what we are looking for. I am aware of what you are offering. I will call you if we need your assistance.	I have told you three times: I will call you if we need your assistance.

Indefinite boundary:	Definite boundary:	Stronger boundary:
I don't think I am ready to make this decision.	I am not ready to make this decision. I will get back to you when I am ready.	I have told you three times: I will call you when I am ready.
I need a little more time to consider it.	I am busy right now. I will call you next week.	I have told you three times. I will call you back next week.
I'm sorry but I am really not interested.	I considered your request, and I am not interested.	I have told you three times: I am not interested.
This is not really a very good time.	This is not a good time for me. Call back next month.	I have told you three times: Call back next month.

You can learn to set limits more decisively by role-playing and reading this list out loud. You should practice expressing strength without depending on anger or frustration to pump up your message. The most powerful way to assert yourself with a man is to express yourself with such confidence that you don't need to back it up with reasons, explanations, or negative emotions.

Men in the workplace can review this list and learn to interpret a woman's boundaries even when she sounds indefinite. He needs to recognize when she is politely trying to say no to his work proposal. By respecting her "polite rejection" and backing off, she will feel respected and may be more willing to consider his proposal at another time. Being pushy will only make matters worse for him.

Learning to Persist

Just as men need to learn how to back off and respect a boundary, women need to learn how to demonstrate persistence and ask again. When a man resists her requests or says no in some manner, it is not always final. A woman needs to practice hearing a "no" and then ask again as if for the first time. By not feeling rejected she can then persist in a friendly manner.

This is good practice for preparing to ask for a raise or more substantial support. Without this kind of practice, it may be hard for her to hear no and not feel blocked when she asks for something. Her discomfort with hearing no makes it hard for her to negotiate or take less in a friendly manner. Women who have learned to hear a "no" as "not yet" become great negotiators and are greatly admired by men.

> **Women who have learned to hear a "no" as "not yet" become great negotiators.**

The more a woman gets personally upset when her request is not met, the more difficult it will be for her to negotiate what she can get. Often if a woman gets a no, she will not ask again for a long time. Instead, she needs to hear this rejection as a "not yet" or "I'll think about it." By listening in a nonoffended manner to what might be said along with this rejection, she can begin to negotiate, either asking for less or a plan for getting more. Instead of negotiating in this persistent manner, many women back up their requests by describing the problems they have had to overcome or how much they have to do, which makes them look even less professional.

A wise man in a similar situation will avoid appearing as if he is complaining and will objectively point out his achievements and the benefits he has provided the company. If plan A doesn't work, he will move on to plan B and negotiate for less. The process of negotiation proceeds by restating what you want in a variety of different ways that will be more acceptable to the other party but also give you more of what you want. It is important to enter a negotiation with several alternative plans. By not taking rejection personally, you are able to stay flexible. When a boss senses that you are not taking offense, he doesn't have to get defensive, and he will stay flexible as well.

Men or women who have played sports often get a lot more practice with rejection and failure in life. By playing sports, they are used to striking out in one inning and then scoring a point in the next. With this experience, they instinctively know that persistence is a sign of confidence. If he or she is on the bench and wanting to get back in the game, by continuing to ask, his or her chances of convincing the coach go up.

> **A man takes rejection as "later,"**
> **and a woman hears a rigid no.**

"If at first you don't succeed then try, try again" is an old saying from Mars. For a man, asking for a raise is like sitting on the bench in a basketball game and asking the coach to get back in the game. In a friendly way, half expecting rejection, a man will ask again and again to get in the game. He will say things like, "I can do it. I know I can do it. Come on, let me get out there."

A man in the workplace does the same thing. He is always on a campaign to let the boss know that he is the guy for the promotion or raise. In a variety of ways, he sends this message:

"I am the right guy for this job. I can do it. I will do a great job. Look at what I have done. Look at these achievements. I really want it. See how much I want it. I will do what it takes. I know that I can do it. I will not let you down. You can count on me."

In this way he is preparing the boss to give him a raise. It is this same attitude that makes a decision maker accept a proposal. If the presenter is confident, then it helps the decision maker feel more confident as well.

With this detached, undemanding attitude a clear message is given. He is saying, "I want more, and I also appreciate what I get. I want more, because I feel I deserve more, but I am willing to do what it takes to prove it to you or earn it. I want more and think when you see what I can do or have done you will be willing to give me more."

A male or female boss with Martian characteristics is much more inclined to give more when he or she senses that the employee really wants more. Often in negotiations women get less because the decision maker senses that she will settle for less. This message is expressed by her tone and choice of words.

A male or female boss with Venusian characteristics is more inclined to give more when he or she senses that the employee deserves more. Often in negotiations with a Venusian boss a persistent employee, male or female, will get less because he or she sounds too pushy and demanding.

On Venus, they are raised to be nice, sharing, and supportive. One of the ways they are taught to be nice is to take the broken cookie and offer to others the best cookies. This sacrificing and self-effacing attitude makes for great nurturing skills, but it doesn't help in negotiating for more from a Martian boss.

Girls are taught to be nice by taking the broken cookie and offering others the best cookies.

A man demonstrates his ambition for more while being careful to not complain. In a positive manner, he makes it known again and again in a variety of ways that he wants more. Every time he advertises his success in order to stand out, a male boss or supervisor takes notice and can clearly see that he really wants more.

A man will directly ask for the promotion with a clear tone of voice that indicates, "I can handle it if you need time to think about it or if you don't think I am ready." His positive tone indicates, "I trust that you will see all that I do and then reward me with a raise or some increased benefits." In this way, a man may only directly ask a few times, but then as the positive reports keep coming in the boss will be thinking about whether he wants to give a raise.

If a man or woman asks for a raise and can't handle the rejection in a positive manner, then the boss may get defensive and instead of looking for reasons to eventually give a raise, he will look for reasons to justify not giving a raise.

Negotiating a Raise

Learning how to ask for more is a big part of negotiating a raise, but standing up and standing out is the basis of getting more. Many women assume that someone is going to knock on their door, having noticed how hard they have been working. As a result they will be given a promotion, a salary increase, or some extra bonus or perk. This may happen on Venus, but it doesn't happen on Mars.

Without this insight, a woman in the workplace may see others getting these benefits and just assume that she will get the same when her work is recognized and appreciated. She continues working hard, assuming that recognition will automatically come when her work is appreciated. When recognition doesn't come or when she doesn't get the promotion, then she feels unappreciated and a feeling of resentment comes up.

What she has to know is that she may be appreciated, but if she doesn't actively promote herself and then ask in a way that works, she will not get the recognition that she deserves. Some women make the mistake of thinking that if they are liked they will have a greater chance of getting ahead. This is true in some ways but not in others. It is certainly harder to get a raise if you are not liked. But more important than being personally liked is being assertive about asking. Being liked because you are nice doesn't earn promotions and raises.

Many bosses and managers appreciate employees who don't ask for more benefits or salary increases. Who wouldn't feel more at ease if an employee did a good job and didn't ask for much? That is a good deal. When you get a good deal at the store, you don't offer to pay more because you like the store. In a similar manner, just because a boss likes a woman or she does a good job, he will not necessarily offer to pay her more.

> **Just because a boss likes a woman,
> he will not necessarily offer to pay her more.**

From a boss's perspective it is a comfort to know that he or she doesn't have to give everyone more. She already is having to deal with other more "Martian" employees who are persistently asking for more. Every business struggles with the bottom line to increase profit. If she doesn't have to pay more in salaries, then it is easier for her to have higher profit margins.

In the workplace people don't necessarily offer you what you are worth. Imagine putting your house on the market and saying, "Just give me your best offer" or "Give me what you can comfortably afford." If you used this approach, you would never get close to the market value.

> **In the workplace people don't simply offer you what
> you are worth; you have to negotiate your value.**

No one ever *wants* to pay more. You wouldn't decide to buy a house and offer to pay more just because you really loved the house. In a similar way, the workplace will pay you what they have to pay you. They *will* pay more, but they need a little nudging. Those who get raises have often learned how to stand up and stand out and negotiate to get those raises and advancements. They give clear messages that they really want it.

Desire, Worthiness, and Confidence

Sustaining a strong desire while projecting a sense of worthiness and confidence increases your ability to negotiate. Complaining is seen on Mars as desire without confidence. Women often feel entitled but dissatisfied by what they are getting. When a male boss hears dissatisfaction, he hears complaining and will begin to withdraw his respect. The secret for negotiating a raise or promotion is to stay positive and avoid complaining.

This prejudice in the workplace is not just toward women, it is also toward men who don't assert themselves in a positive manner. A boss will have a greater awareness of an employee's desire and worthiness for a promotion or an advance when that employee makes his wishes and achievements clearly known without complaining. To motivate a boss to give more, an employee must radiate a desire for more and a sense of worthiness that comes from confidence.

**To motivate a boss to give more,
an employee must radiate desire and confidence.**

Both men and women can increase their opportunity to get more when they understand a boss's perspective. This applies not only in seeking a promotion or raise but while making any kind of presentation or proposal to a decision maker. The boss or decision maker doesn't easily say yes. They need to be convinced by the person making the presentation. They look for reassurance that they are making the best deal. They certainly don't want to make a mistake. If the presenter seems unsure or not definite, then the decision maker begins to feel unsure and indefinite. If the presenter is confident and positive, then the decision maker feels more assured.

In asking for a raise one must pick the right time. There needs to be a lot of preparation so that the employer is aware of your achievements. Don't wait until you are asking for a promotion to make your successes known. When you ask for a raise, your boss should already be aware of your accomplishments.

In the process of advertising your accomplishments, do it simply because you are taking credit where credit is due and not because you are hoping to get a promotion. Asking for more, too often, will make you appear needy. Any boss, male or female, needs time to consider promotions and advances. The more you make them aware of your efforts and accomplishments the more prepared they will be to recognize your worth when you seek to negotiate a raise.

While asking for a raise you have to be reasonable. On the one hand, you need to ask for what you want, but on the other hand, if you ask for too much it may cause you to lose your job. It is easy to burn bridges or offend others by asking for too much.

The secret for asking is to ask for more in small increments, and do it in a way that is nondemanding. If you ask for more in a way that says you really *need* more, then if you don't get it, a boss may feel you are not right for the job. The boss needs to be assured that you appreciate what he's offering. He or she reasons that if the present compensation is not enough to meet your needs, then it is the wrong job for you.

**If you ask for too much it may
cause you to lose your job.**

When asking for a raise, men or women should first review their achievements and the results they have produced for the company. Having focused on the benefits of their work, they have laid a foundation to ask for more. A wise man or woman asks for more in a tone and manner that says, "I appreciate what I am getting and the results I have produced deserve more compensation," or "The market has changed, people doing my job are getting more today." This kind of objective approach is always better than, "I am working too hard for this kind of pay." Or "I need more money to pay my rent or mortgage."

A man or woman who gets ahead will always be jockeying around so that his or her achievements are seen and recognized by the boss. He will send copies of flattering letters and send glowing reports of achievements. By making her achievements known long before she asks for a raise, a woman will be much more successful in her negotiations.

To Ask or Not to Ask

On Venus, the quality of her relationships really is more important than the money she makes. Rather than risk offending her boss or client, a woman will appear much more accepting and accommodating by holding back from asking for more. As a result women are more reserved about asking for more and often get less. Knowing when to ask, how to ask, and how much to ask for is challenging for everyone. With a greater understanding of what your boss may be thinking, then asking for more becomes easier.

The bottom line of any negotiation is to determine what a person will accept. If you sell your car and say you will accept anywhere between $15,000 and $18,000, it would be absurd for someone to call up and say, OK, I like this car so much I will give you $18,000. They would offer the lowest price that you would accept. That is the nature of business and a free economy. It is not the way they do things on Venus, but it is the way most bosses, male or female, think. To get more you have to ask for it.

On Venus, unless a woman feels resentful, she doesn't want to appear too demanding. It is not nice to want more. As a result, sometimes it is only when a woman already feels resentful that she will experience a persistent nagging inside that says, "I am doing more for this company, so I deserve to get paid more." Or "Now that I have proved my value to this company, I deserve to get paid more." One difference between men and women is that men will often feel this way long before they feel resentful.

When a woman sees others getting more and her getting less, she may begin to feel resentful and then demand more. The problem with this approach is that male bosses don't respond well to emotionally charged ultimatums. Bosses are not heartless, but they do need some motivation to pay more and give more. This takes time. An axiom in sales is that a person needs to hear about a product seven times before being motivated to consider purchasing it.

> **Bosses are not heartless, but they do need some motivation to pay more and give more.**

Repetition is the secret of getting what you want. When a woman asks for a raise or promotion, the first time she should recognize that she is just beginning the process. It would be very inappropriate to make a demand. When you want more, you need to patiently promote yourself again and again.

When a woman asks for more and doesn't get it, she may not realize that if she is gracious about not getting more, then she can immediately ask for something less. At the very least she can work out a plan that would eventually lead her to getting what she wants. This is the art of negotiation.

Instead of walking out with a no, she can walk out of a negotiation with at least something to appreciate. Male bosses are particularly motivated to give more later when what they give in the present time is appreciated. When a Martian asks for a raise, if he doesn't get it then he will ask for some lesser benefit and then show a lot of appreciation. In this way by being happy to take less he opens a door to keep getting more.

> **If a man doesn't get what he has asked for,**
> **he will ask for some lesser benefit**
> **and then show a lot of appreciation.**

One of the biggest mistakes a woman may make when negotiating a raise is to justify her request with an exploration of her personal dissatisfaction. Often, when asking for a raise or some benefit of support, a woman will lose support by talking about how much she does and how little she gets. By pointing out how hard she is working or how difficult things are for her she sabotages her request.

This "sharing" is often expressed in the emotional tone of being overwhelmed or exhausted. On Venus this would communicate how dedicated, hardworking, and caring she is. On her planet and with a Venusian boss, her feelings will evoke both an admiration and an empathetic response from her boss. As a result she will get the support she needs. But on Mars, or with a Martian boss, by expressing her negative feelings and sharing her problems she loses points and gets less support.

Even if her boss is more Venusian, instead of wanting to give her more money, he or she will feel more motivated to lighten her load and give her less to do. Her boss may conclude that if she can't handle the load she is carrying now, she can't handle more. With this perspective it is hard for a boss to think of giving her a raise. The support she gets may be a few suggestions about how to handle things better.

To earn equal respect as demonstrated through raises and promotions, it is essential that when women ask for more, they don't use their emotions to justify their request. Expressing a little negative emotion to elicit the reassurance of a coworker may be appropriate, but to burden your boss with these feelings and expect him or her to reciprocate with a raise is unrealistic. By staying positive by focusing on her successes, achievements, contributions, increased efficiency, and increased productivity a woman will have an extra advantage in negotiating for more.

Vulnerability in the Workplace

Once while making a job recommendation for a woman who had worked for my company, I was surprised to hear a woman ask me very directly, "Has she ever cried under pressure?" It was clear that from this woman's perspective, she didn't want to hire a woman who would cry in the workplace. At first this seemed cruel and heartless, but I gradually realized a grain of wisdom in what this woman was saying. I would certainly not fire a woman because she cried at work, but I would not encourage her to use the workplace to get that kind of support.

It is important that we don't focus on getting our emotional needs met in the workplace. Crying is one of the many ways a man or woman will open up to receive the emotional support of others. This kind of vulnerability is most appropriately expressed in our personal relationships. It is inappropriate to look to your boss or coworker as a shoulder to cry on. The workplace should not be a substitute family, lover, or therapist.

A Venusian boss or coworker would be more comfortable with displays of vulnerability, but a Martian is not. A woman who cries or expresses vulnerable feelings in the workplace sets a man up to be the bad guy. If he doesn't consider and respond to her tender feelings with compassion and support, he could be viewed as callous and insensitive. This is not fair to him and is a sign that she is expecting too much from him and the workplace. Though his human tendency is to comfort her, it is important to stifle the impulse and not take on the role of therapist or family member.

**A woman who cries or expresses vulnerable feelings
in the workplace sets a man up to be the bad guy.**

Rather than reaching out to hug her, he can hand her a tissue or offer to get her a glass of water. He should then resume the conversation without paying any attention to the crying. He can get back to business as if it didn't happen. To give it attention either encourages that kind of display of emotion or makes him appear more insensitive when he finally has to shift the subject back to the task at hand. Asking concerned questions just makes it harder for her to resume control. It is not his job to comfort or counsel her, that is her responsibility. By offering life-enrichment programs and counseling programs, a boss or company can provide a more appropriate kind of support.

If a male boss or coworker assumes the role of comforter, he may cause a series of possible problems that a woman boss in the role of comforter would instinctively avoid. A man tends to become overly responsible and give special treatment. By doing this he then sets a precedent. Unless he continues to meet her need for his sensitive side, she will eventually begin to resent that his business decisions are primarily based on the bottom line. If he continues to be sensitive and compassionate toward her, other employees will resent the favoritism. Ultimately, if she begins to depend on the workplace to resolve her personal problems or satisfy her personal needs, he will begin to resent her for becoming so needy and lose respect for her.

He may feel as if he is "forced to be nice" to her because she is so sensitive. She may get his empathy but she will clearly not get the promotion or advance she wants. With this insight a woman can be most successful by keeping her personal needs separate from what she expects to get in the workplace.

In the workplace crying may get a man's empathy but she risks not getting the promotion or advance she wants.

This same dynamic applies when men or women use sex to get ahead. With sex, they may seduce their boss into giving special favors but it is always temporary. When the flush of romance has faded, their boss will pull back his or her special attention and resent feeling obligated to give special consideration. Not only do other employees feel resentful, but so will their boss.

Sexual Harassment

Just as expressing vulnerable feelings in the workplace is inappropriate, so is the expression of sexual feelings. Women more commonly display emotional vulnerability in an inappropriate manner, but men more often express their personal needs for sexual stimulation in an inappropriate manner. Just as crying should be left for more intimate relationships outside the workplace, so should sex.

There will always be some degree of sexual expression in the workplace. After all, for many men and women who work sixty hours a week, the workplace is their primary place to search for and find a romantic partner. Without an understanding of our different sensitivities, both men and women behave in ways that are sometimes inappropriate.

Today, with so much media attention on criminal sexual harassment cases, there is confusion regarding what is appropriate and what is not. The term "sexual harassment" means many different things to different people. Just because a woman feels harassed by a man, it doesn't mean his behavior is criminal. Sexual harassment cases are thrown out of court every day. At the same time, just because a man thinks his sexual behavior is innocent, it doesn't mean he is innocent in a court of law.

**The term "sexual harassment" means
many different things to different people.**

For some people, "sexual harassment" means inappropriate sexual comments, advances, or behaviors that are offensive or not welcome. For others, it means different degrees of rape and the criminal abuse of power to satisfy one's own sexual urges or needs. With such a range of interpretations, it is important to clarify the expression "sexual harassment" and recognize that some sexual behaviors are inappropriate and thus worthy of a reprimand, while other behaviors are punishable as a crime.

In our discussion, we will limit ourselves to understanding the feelings of harassment that occur from behaviors that are worthy of reprimand, and not criminal behaviors like rape and the abuse of power. It is important to recognize that there is a distinction between inappropriate behavior that is annoying to others and criminal behavior that is abusive. As men and women both learn to identify and correct annoying and inappropriate sexual behavior, it becomes easier to avoid and protect against more serious behaviors that constitute criminal sexual harassment.

**Sexual harassment can be lessened by recognizing
the difference between inappropriate behavior
that is annoying and criminal behavior that is abusive.**

Both men and women commonly make inappropriate sexual advances, but men have a greater tendency to persist in sexual behavior even though a woman has expressed her resistance. The more he persists, the more unwelcome sexual expressions, such as sexual jokes, advances, and comments, shift from being sources of annoyance to abuse. A man will often make light of her resistance and not take it seriously. Or he will resent her disapproval and alienate her. Either way this disrespect will make her feel harassed.

A man must recognize that when a woman makes it clear that his sexual behavior is not welcome, and he persists against her will, she will feel harassed. Although he may not consider this to be a violation of her rights, it is. Even though a behavior may not constitute criminal harassment, it will create mistrust and resentment in their working relationship. It will negate his attempts to have a positive and cooperative work environment.

To avoid generating feelings of sexual harassment, a man requires a greater sensitivity of awareness that respects a woman's reactions to his sexual behaviors even though they are different from his.

> **With greater understanding of women, a man can accept**
> **that a woman's reactions to sex are different.**

A woman can also benefit from this exploration. By understanding why a man might ignore her resistance, and in some cases resent her disapproval, she can be more effective in setting her boundaries.

Setting Sexual Boundaries

Without an understanding of her perspective, when a woman sets her sexual boundaries or complains of sexual harassment, some men may conclude that she is making a big deal out of nothing. He reasons he would welcome a little sexual attention and so concludes that she should as well. He thinks he is just having a little fun and dismisses her resistance. When she feels offended by unwanted advances or talk, he doesn't understand.

> **A man reasons he would welcome a little sexual**
> **attention and so concludes a woman should as well.**

This kind of thinking is a carryover from the past, when women were not allowed by society to like sex. This prohibition of a more puritanical age put men in the awkward position of having to persist, despite a woman's resistance. Some women would say no, but really welcomed a man's persistence. This old way of relating is no longer appropriate. Women today are free to like sex and when they say no they mean it.

These are six common reasons men persist in unwanted sexual behavior or have difficulty in validating a woman's feelings of harassment. In the second column there are reasons to assist a man in respecting a woman's right to set her sexual boundaries.

Why Men Resist Sexual Boundaries

A man's reasoning:	Understanding her reactions:
He thinks his behavior is just innocent flirting. He reasons, "What is wrong with flirting? Other women don't have a problem with it."	A man needs to recognize that just because a behavior is okay for one person it doesn't make it okay for another. Harassment is not so much about the behavior, but because he persists when she is not asking for it.
He defends his actions like this: "If a woman admired my body, even if I wasn't sexually interested in her, I wouldn't feel harassed. I would like it or at least feel flattered."	Women respond differently to sexual stimulation. They have a whole different set of hormonal and emotional reactions associated with sex. Unless she feels emotionally attracted to him, his sexual attention is not stimulating. What is stimulating to him may be annoying to her.

A man's reasoning:

On his planet, behaviors like hanging pornography on the wall or the expression of sexual jokes are not offensive. He thinks she is overreacting.

He thinks he is reciprocating her sexual advances. When a woman dresses in a way that accentuates her sexual attractiveness or she casually touches him in a social interaction, he may think she is initiating a sexual interaction.

When she resists him in a tentative, nice, or friendly manner, he assumes she is wanting him to pursue her.

When she feels harassed, because sexual harassment can also describe a criminal act, he resents being put in the category with a criminal rapist or pervert. As a result he reacts defensively and dismisses her feelings of harassment as overreaction.

Understanding her reactions:

On her planet, these behaviors are offensive. It is not fair for him to say, "My way is the right way." He can hang his pornography at home or make his jokes with men around.

On Venus, they casually touch (in nonsexual zones) as a way of connecting. It is not a sign that she is flirting. She may be dressing to attract a man, but that doesn't mean she is wanting to attract you.

Women today are liberated. If they want a sexual interaction they will clearly say yes. If she seems unsure or tentative in her resistance, she is saying no, but being careful to not hurt your feelings.

It is not her fault that society is confused about harassment. Don't justify your own defensive reaction by blaming her. Validate her feelings of harassment and give her the respect she deserves by adjusting your behaviors toward her.

Throughout *How To Get What You Want in the Workplace* we have explored how men and women react differently to the same situations. With this new insight, it is not a great stretch of the mind to realize or at least accept that what he welcomes sexually, she may be repelled by. What stimulates him may be disgusting to her.

To avoid generating feelings of harassment, men need to remember that we are from different planets. Likewise, with a greater understanding of the way men think, a woman can be more successful in setting her boundaries to avoid being sexually harassed.

Why Sexual Attention Can Be Disturbing

Some men question why sexual attention or comments can be so disturbing to a woman because they have not walked in her shoes and experienced life from her perspective. By exploring the many reasons a man doesn't relate to the feeling of harassment, it can assist a man in getting a glimpse of her world. This insight is helpful to create the compassion and sensitivity required to freely adjust his behaviors. The following six points explain why a man doesn't relate to a woman's experience:

1. He doesn't share the uncomfortable experience of being appreciated as a sex object instead of having her competence and intelligence recognized.

2. He has not spent much of his life trying to be polite while saying no to unwanted advances.

3. He has not experienced being the object of sexual prejudice, having to prove that she can do a job just as effectively as a man.

4. He doesn't consider how challenging it is to have an ongoing harmonious work relationship with someone you have to keep rejecting.

5. When a woman doesn't choose to cooperate with a man's sexual banter or requests, she could then be treated as an outsider, a prude, a "stick in the mud," or too serious, and this is unfair to her.

6. By setting her boundaries she may have to deal with his anger or indifference. Most disturbing to her is the feeling of exclusion that results as well as feeling powerless to correct the situation.

Many big companies have their own policies when it comes to protecting their workers and themselves from sexual harassment lawsuits. Without an understanding of our differences some male employees resent these restrictions. These six insights can help release the resentment a man may feel when he has to restrain himself, to be respectful of the opposite sex. By understanding a woman's different perspective, a man begins to feel that restricting sexual advances and banter is both fair and reasonable.

Saying No to Sexual Advances

A woman can also be part of the solution as well. Sometimes harassment occurs because a man doesn't get a clear message to stop. By learning to clearly set her boundaries without getting upset, she may easily motivate him to stop without any negative repercussions. Every day, savvy women stop men's advances long before they need to seek help from management.

Sometimes a woman's feelings about a man are hard for him to read. As a result he makes a pass to find out the answer. Some women can easily laugh it off with a comment like, "Nah, I don't feel that way about you, you're my good buddy!" or "Come on, you're like my brother!" For most men, this kind of comment will stop his advances while also helping him to save face.

When a man makes a pass, if a woman is not interested, she

needs to give a friendly but definite message. She should not sound unsure when she means no. Often a woman doesn't realize that by setting an "indefinite" boundary regarding a man's sexual behavior, comments, or attention, some men just don't hear "no" or "stop." Certainly, if her assertive communication doesn't work, she should seek help.

By practicing being more direct, a woman can get much better results in setting her boundaries. If attempting to be "nice" by setting a less definite boundary doesn't work, without getting angry, she should then express a more definite boundary. Although it may seem rude on her planet, men respect clear and definite boundaries. What men have difficulty with is hearing boundaries and anger at the same time. By staying calm and centered her effectiveness is increased.

After repeating a more definite boundary, if he still doesn't respect her, then she should move on to a stronger boundary. If this doesn't work she should definitely seek help. Here are some examples of what she can say:

Assertive Communication about Sex

Less definite boundary:	Definite boundary:	Stronger boundary:
I don't really like that kind of fooling around.	I am really not interested. Find someone else to entertain.	I have told you three times. Find someone else to entertain.
I admire you but as a friend.	You are not my type. Let's just be friends.	I have told you three times. You are not my type.

Less definite boundary:	Definite boundary:	Stronger boundary:
Right now I am involved with someone.	I'm not available and I am not interested in having a relationship with you.	I have told you three times. I am not interested in having a relationship with you. Find someone else.
I am really busy right now. I have a lot on my plate.	I keep my personal life separate from my work life. I am not interested in having a relationship with you.	I have told you three times. I am not interested in having a relationship with you. Stop calling me.
Excuse me, I didn't mean to give the wrong idea.	You are being pushy. I am not interested in having a relationship with you.	I have told you three times. I want you to respect my wishes. I am not available.
I'm sorry, but I am seeing someone else.	I am not interested in starting a relationship with you.	I have told you three times. I am not interested in having a relationship with you. Stop trying.

When setting a boundary, it becomes more powerful and clear when a woman doesn't get upset, cast judgment, give lectures, or give threats. In addition, she should not give additional information about her personal life to justify her response. No explanation is required. If she seeks to comfort him, then he assumes that she cares for him and he continues to persist.

The secret of assertiveness is to be brief and don't use emotional tones or feelings to console or to back up your request. When a man seems pushy or belligerent, she can be more successful by setting a limit without letting him experience that he is annoying her or getting to her. The less she becomes emotional the less he needs to defend his actions and can back off. By not getting emotional he can save face, and change his behavior.

Setting the Boundary Between the Workplace and Our Personal Life

Just because a woman dresses in a provocative way it is not an invitation for a man to express himself in a sexual manner. A woman has a right to be attractive and dress in whatever manner that makes her feel good. Her style in dressing doesn't justify a man's unwanted and unsolicited advances or comments.

> **A woman's style in dressing doesn't justify a man's unsolicited sexual advances or comments.**

When a man has pictures of his wife and family in his office, that is his statement that he is a loving and caring person. It isn't an invitation for everyone to come in his office and cry on his shoulder. Just as both men and women are expected to leave their personal feelings to their personal life, they should also delegate sexual feelings to their personal life and separate them from the workplace.

This does not mean that a woman "should" never display vulnerable emotions, or a man should never display sexual attention. Both behaviors can be quite acceptable if the other person is receptive and it does not consume work time.

A man's flirtatious behavior becomes offensive when it is not welcome. If a woman is interested in having a relationship with a man, then the same behavior would be fine. Likewise with a woman. If the man she is sharing feelings with happens to be very close to her, then becoming more vulnerable may be appropriate.

There is no clear-cut, black-and-white definition of what is right when it comes to sex and vulnerability in the workplace. The best way to approach this potential problem is to be cautious and considerate of others. By clearly setting your own boundaries, and by respecting the boundaries of others, you will be maintaining a professional attitude.

10

Minimizing Stress with Emotional Support

Understanding differences goes a long way to minimizing stress, but it cannot replace your need for emotional support. It feels particularly uncomfortable when everyone else is getting what they need and you are not. In the past, primarily women felt this way, but more and more, as different areas of the workplace are populated by women, men also feel frustrated and sometimes unwelcome. Today, both men and women require a greater degree of emotional support.

No matter how much a man tries to be supportive of a woman, at times she still needs the caring, empathetic support another woman can instinctively provide. Likewise, a man will feel a certain ease when other men are around. We all need times when we can be ourselves without feeling the need to edit or change our behavior. Being outnumbered by the opposite sex can be an uncomfortable experience for both men and women. This challenge can be overcome by making sure that outside the workplace we are able to get our unfulfilled personal needs met.

**We all need times when we can be ourselves without
feeling the need to edit or change our behavior.**

There will always be challenging situations in the workplace
in which we cannot get our personal needs met. Unless we can
take action to get what we need, this becomes a breeding ground
for resentment. If we keep trying to get support where it is not
possible, we will become increasingly frustrated. Instead of looking to the workplace for support, we need to go elsewhere. By
knowing where to get your needs fulfilled, the tendency to blame
your job or others in the workplace decreases. As a result, stress
decreases and positive feelings of confidence and appreciation
increase.

Stress and Lost Productivity

Companies that are more supportive of family life, by providing
more flexible schedules when needed and various life-enrichment
programs, have experienced immediate positive results; productivity and profits have dramatically increased. When employees
are more emotionally fulfilled they are naturally more motivated,
creative, productive, and cooperative.

It is not stress, but the way we cope with stress, that determines our level of productivity. By making sure we get our emotional needs met we are better prepared to meet the stressful
challenges of work. If we are getting the emotional support we
need, the stress of the workplace stimulates greater creativity and
energy. Stress only results in lost productivity when our emotional needs are not being met.

**It is not stress, but the way we cope with stress, that
determines our level of productivity.**

The inability to cope with stress causes workers to make mistakes, which wastes time and money. Unhappy employees tend to create a lot of unnecessary emotional tension and conflict. Any company directly benefits by supporting a more enriched personal life for their employees.

In the bigger picture the relaxed and personally fulfilled employee makes the best decisions. It is not longer hours of work, but more efficient hours of work, that makes the greatest difference.

The most successful people are the ones who are able to minimize the negative effects of stress. The more our emotional needs are supported, the better we are at coping with stress. For some people the challenge of the workplace completely nourishes them, but for most it is having a personal life outside the workplace.

How Men React Under Stress

Both men and women react differently to stress. On Mars, when a man is not getting his emotional needs met, he will tend to become overly focused and lose productivity by isolating himself in his cave. While interacting with others he will have a greater tendency to grumble and resist helpful input or assistance. His increased aggressiveness and irritability are signs that he is overstressed.

Under stress a man will become overly focused and lose productivity by isolating himself in his cave.

In this state, most men are not even aware that they have become overly focused. They experience a kind of tunnel vision and cannot see the bigger picture. By focusing on the big fire that urgently needs to be put out, a man ignores the other little fires that also need to be attended to. Unless a problem or task is at the top of his priority list, he doesn't give it importance. It is all or nothing. By ignoring activities of a lesser priority, these little issues eventually become much bigger problems. Certainly there is a time and place to ignore everything and focus on the emergency, but when this tendency becomes chronic, productivity is reduced along with the quality of all his work relationships.

When overly stressed, men experience a kind of tunnel vision and cannot see the bigger picture.

When men are overly stressed, they also have a greater tendency to immediately blame others instead of being accountable and responsible. Not only does this tendency minimize his flexibility and creativity, but he becomes very intimidating to others. Most of his relationship skills and manners go out the window when he is focused on his task.

With an awareness of these tendencies, a man can compensate by attempting to be more considerate of others and more accountable for his mistakes. At such times, he needs to force himself to expand his awareness and create time to attend to the smaller fires that also need to be put out. This requires a lot of effort because his tendency is to remain focused on that "one thing" that is causing him the most stress.

Most importantly, he needs to reduce the effects of stress by taking some time to meet his emotional needs. Instead of isolating himself and focusing on his work task, he needs to do something relaxing and fulfilling. By balancing his work and personal life he can avoid wasting time and money and increase his productivity.

How Women React under Stress

When a woman is overly stressed she tends to have the opposite reaction than a man. Women become overly expansive and feel increasingly overwhelmed by how much needs to be done. She will lose productivity by feeling a greater need to talk about problems rather than solving them. She will tend to blame herself. This self-blaming tendency increases her self-doubt and blocks her from asserting herself and her needs.

In this overwhelmed state, when she needs help the most, she will instead take on more responsibilities. Her ability to clearly identify her priorities is lessened and much time can be wasted on putting out little fires while the big fire is not being attended to. Little problems may seem much bigger that they are. In a state of feeling overwhelmed it is much harder to make decisions.

> **When overly stressed, women experience**
> **a sense of being overwhelmed and little problems seem**
> **bigger than they are.**

Certainly there is a time and place to focus on all the little issues that are not being attended to, but when this tendency is chronic and a woman feels burdened by all that has to be done then her effectiveness and productivity are limited. Feeling overwhelmed or exhausted is a clear indication that she is not getting her emotional needs met.

As her awareness of problems and responsibilities increases, she will begin to feel increasing exhaustion because "it is all too much to do." Unless corrected, this feeling of exhaustion turns into resentment that she doesn't get enough support.

> **Unless corrected, this feeling of exhaustion eventually**
> **turns into resentment.**

At a time when she needs to take more time to relax and get the emotional support she needs, she will instead feel guilty taking time for herself. Instead of taking more time to meet her personal needs she will take on more to do. Unless she is adept in meeting her emotional needs, when she does take some time off, she will worry more and be unable to relax and get the support she needs.

Women have an extra nurturing gene and they often give to everyone else and forget their own personal needs. In most cases, when a woman is overly stressed, she needs to first create more support in her personal life, and then she is better able to sort out her priorities and stresses at work.

By taking time to talk with friends about the sources of her stress, a woman can most effectively cope with it. If she takes work time to do this, she will not only waste time but may alienate coworkers who want to use their time more productively. Talking about problems to reduce stress primarily works in a context that doesn't require a solution to the problem. Certainly a little venting and sharing of problems in the workplace is helpful and effective to minimize stress, but it does not replace the need for a personal life.

With an awareness of these tendencies, a woman can recognize the symptoms of stress and take time to meet her emotional needs outside the workplace. By talking with friends who are not involved in her work life, her stress is more effectively released. With this relief, she can then begin to create more balance in her life and make sure that she is prioritizing her emotional needs.

The Workplace Is Not Therapy

The bottom line for both men and women is that the workplace is not responsible for your personal fulfillment. That is up to you. If your job is not providing the emotional support you need, blaming the company will not make your situation any better. If you experience severe symptoms of stress, then until you can start to create that support in your personal life, you may benefit from therapy. Don't expect the workplace to be that therapy. If you get help from the workplace, then consider that a dessert.

As long as we regard the workplace as a parent, friend, therapist, or love partner, we are setting ourselves up for failure and resentment. Whenever you point a finger of blame at the workplace, you become a part of the problem and not a part of the solution.

> **If we expect the workplace to be a parent, friend,**
> **therapist, or love partner,**
> **we set ourselves up for failure and resentment.**

Change in the workplace is needed, but to create this change we must make sure our requirements are reasonable. All change occurs in small steps. When one step works, then another can occur. When personal resentment is out of the way, we are in a much better position to hear the needs of others as we express our own. This mutual respect and appreciation is the basis of successful negotiation.

Personal resentment dissolves when meeting your needs is not dependent on changing others in the workplace. If you blame a manager, coworker, or the whole opposite sex for your unhappiness, you are giving them free rent in your mind to torment you. Taking responsibility for your fulfillment frees you from being stressed by others with whom you may have to work with. By taking action to find personal fulfillment outside the workplace, you are better equipped to create positive change.

> **Taking responsibility frees you from being stressed by**
> **others with whom you may have to work.**

Ultimately, the ideal attitude for the workplace is to come to work to be nourished by giving support and not by receiving it. In a perfect world, our personal relationships support us while our work relationships challenge us to give support. It is not healthy to depend on work to meet all our personal needs. When we expect the workplace to satisfy these needs, we will be repeatedly disappointed and feel resentful. This attitude will make the workplace even more unpleasant and stressful.

We need always to remember that our job is "just a job." This doesn't mean that we don't strive to do our best, but it does mean that we don't make work more important than having a personal life.

Learning to Give Support

Success is not dependent on receiving emotional support from the workplace, but it is dependent on our ability to give emotional support. In every interaction, one either feels supported or not. When all things are equal, the emotional support we provide is often what will make the difference between success and failure.

For example, if I can buy a new computer on-line or at three different stores in my area for about the same price, how I feel about a particular vender will determine with whom I choose to do business. When a job opportunity is available and five different people are equally qualified, it is just a "good feeling" or "gut feeling" that determines who will be picked.

In the new world market in which there is an abundance of supply, it becomes more important to hone your skills for providing emotional support. The personal alliances you create in the workplace will make the difference between success and failure at all levels of the workplace.

The personal alliances you create in the workplace will make the difference between success and failure.

Understanding our different emotional needs provides a basis for giving support in the workplace more effectively. By understanding the kind of emotional support women need most to minimize stress, a man has an extra tool to effectively give support. Likewise, as women understand what men need to minimize stress, they also have a new advantage in giving support.

This information can be misused. A woman may read what a woman needs and use it to justify her resentment toward the men in her office. A man may read the way men think differently and use that knowledge as an excuse for not making changes in the way he treats women. Avoid having a victim attitude. Don't use this information to blame others or justify staying the same. Instead, use it to earn the respect and trust of others. By understanding our different emotional needs we can make wiser decisions in determining how to succeed in giving emotional support.

The Twelve Emotional Needs

When it comes to supportive communications in the workplace, the emotional tone conveyed in your speech and actions is what matters. When the tone of your voice or actions meets the emotional need of another, you will lessen that person's stress level and earn their respect and trust. They may not even know why. Often men will say, "I don't know why, but I have a gut feeling about this." Or a woman will say, "It may not make sense, but I have a feeling about this." Our respect and trust, like a river flowing downstream, flows toward those who meet our emotional needs.

We may not be aware of our need for calcium, but when we eat or drink something with calcium we just feel better. In a similar way, everyone in the workplace has emotional needs that are either being met or not. When you are able to meet someone's needs, even if they are unaware of their need, they will respond positively.

There are basically twelve emotional needs. They are caring, trust, understanding, acceptance, respect, appreciation, inclusion, admiration, validation, acknowledgment, reassurance, and encouragement. The enormous task of determining how to give support in the workplace is simplified greatly by understanding what helps men and women cope best with stress. By reviewing the list that follows you can stay focused on giving the kind of support that will be appreciated most.

The Primary Emotional Needs on Mars and Venus

Certainly every man and woman needs all twelve types of support, but under stress, women particularly appreciate six kinds of support and men particularly appreciate the other six. The more stress a person feels the more they will appreciate their particular kind of support.

These needs also change according to the situation. A woman in a role that requires her to give orders or assert herself may tend to be from Mars and appreciate most what a man would. A man who is suddenly about to make a big purchase or feels vulnerable in some way may appreciate most what a woman would. A greater awareness of our different needs will assist you in knowing what kind of emotional support to provide in your style of communicating.

This list helps to remind us of what is more important on Mars or Venus for releasing stress. Without this list, it is easy for a man to give the kind of support he needs and overlook what may be more important to a woman. The same is true for women. Instead of focusing on giving the kind of support she appreciates most, she will be much more successful in giving the support men want most. As stress levels go up, these types of support are needed more. Here are the different emotional needs listed side by side:

Stress Busters for Women :	**Stress Busters for Men:**
1. Caring	Trust
2. Understanding	Acceptance
3. Respect	Appreciation
4. Inclusion	Admiration
5. Validation	Acknowledgment
6. Reassurance	Encouragement

In this list of emotional needs each pairing of emotional needs is also reciprocal. For example, when a man is more *caring* of a woman her automatic response is to *trust* him more. When a woman is more *trusting* of a man, he is automatically more *caring* of her. When a man takes the time to listen and *understand* a woman, she is automatically more *accepting* of him and their differences. When a woman *accepts* a man and doesn't try to change him, he becomes more *understanding* and less judgmental of her or her requests.

In this way all of the different needs are reciprocal. To get a particular kind of support you can just focus on giving the reciprocal kind of support. In the following sections we will explore the reciprocal nature of emotional support in greater detail.

1. She Wants Caring and He Wants Trust

When a man's thoughts, decisions, and actions are influenced by a woman's feelings, needs, and wants, she feels considered or that he cares about her. A caring attitude shows interest and concern that a woman's rights, needs, and requests are being met in a reasonable and timely fashion. When a man takes time to demonstrate his caring and consideration even in little ways, it makes a big difference on Venus. He becomes someone she can depend on and support back. In response, he will receive her trust, which will translate into greater loyalty from clients and customers and increased cooperation with coworkers and management.

When a woman's attitude is open and receptive toward a man, he feels trusted. To express trust on Mars is to believe that a man is doing his best and that he wants to do the best job possible. A trusting attitude does not demand perfection but recognizes that mistakes happen and will give the benefit of the doubt. When a woman's words and reactions convey the emotional tone of trust, a man will automatically respond with greater consideration and caring for her. By recognizing a man's positive intention to do the best he can, a woman is able to bring out the best in him.

2. She Wants Understanding and He Wants Acceptance

When a man listens patiently to a woman without giving solutions right away or interrupting her, she gets the message that he is understanding her. When he presumes to know what she wants or feels, she often feels misunderstood. An understanding attitude doesn't presume to know a person's thoughts, feelings, wishes, and wants; instead he gathers meaning from what is heard and moves toward validating what is being communicated. An understanding attitude tends to be empathetic and compassionate. The more a woman feels understood, the more she will tend to relax and give a man the acceptance that he wants.

When a woman is receptive and open to what a man says he feels accepted. When his mistakes are overlooked or minimized, he gets the acceptance he wants. An accepting attitude does not reject but affirms that he is being favorably received. To be accepting, a woman does not have to agree with or approve of a man's thinking or actions. Acceptance is not the belief that someone is perfect, but an attitude that allows for and even expects a degree of imperfection. A man feels acceptance when a woman is not actively motivated to improve or correct him or does not take offense from his thoughts, feelings, and behavior. An accepting attitude will make a man more willing to be understanding of a woman's thoughts, feelings, needs, and wishes.

3. She Wants Respect and He Wants Appreciation

When a man responds to a woman in a way that acknowledges and prioritizes her rights, wishes, and needs, she feels respected. When his behavior respects her thoughts and feelings, she will begin to experience a heartfelt appreciation for him. Concrete and physical expressions of respect, like immediately doing a task for her or calling back right away, do not go unnoticed. Though this is not so important on Mars, these expressions of respect are greatly appreciated on Venus.

When a woman acknowledges having received personal benefit and value from a man's efforts and behavior, a man feels appreciated. With this insight, a woman can give a man support by simply allowing him to assist her in ways that she will appreciate. This is another good motivator to encourage women to directly ask when they need assistance. When a man is appreciated, he knows that his efforts are not wasted and is encouraged to give more. In response, he becomes more respectful.

4. She Wants Inclusion and He Wants Admiration

When a man actively asks questions to draw a woman into a conversation, she feels included. When a man makes sexual jokes or talks about sports, he creates a sense of separation. When a man offers his assistance without being asked or invites her assistance, she gets the feeling that she is included in a supportive community.

An inclusive attitude acknowledges the relatedness between two or more people. Rather than focusing on differences, it focuses on similarities to create a sense of connection and rapport. When a man seeks to create inclusion by involving a woman in his thinking, planning, and activities, she will automatically respond with an admiration for who he is and what he does.

To admire a man is to regard him with wonder, delight, confidence or pleased approval. He feels admired when she is impressed not only by his competence in doing a task, but by his unique characteristics, skills or talents, which may include strength, persistence, integrity, discipline, honesty, kindness, humor, warmth, and insight. When a man feels admired, he is more willing to collaborate with a woman or include her in developing a project. When a woman is able to recognize a talent or admire a characteristic in a man's behavior, she automatically creates a connection that motivates inclusive behavior on his part. With this kind of support, he feels less of a need to pull away and do things on his own.

5. She Wants Validation and He Wants Acknowledgment

When a man does not object to or argue with a woman's feelings, rights, and wants, but instead accepts and confirms her validity, she is more willing to acknowledge the good in his actions and behaviors. Often a woman feels she has to fight to be heard or to make a difference. When she wants to explore a problem by talking about it and men minimize the problem or offer solutions, they cross a line and she feels invalidated. To validate her perspective does not mean a man has to agree with it. He just has to take the time to see a situation from her perspective. She does not require that he see the situation in the same way. When a man seeks to validate rather than discount, a woman acknowledges his other expressions of support and assistance.

On Mars, they greatly value competence and achievement. Whenever a woman takes time to acknowledge a man's competence or his achievements it is music to his ears. An acknowledging attitude remembers and measures a man based on his achievements and not his failures. It is the opposite of an attitude that says, "What have you done for me lately?" Instead, it recognizes the good in what he has done lately. When a man feels his efforts are acknowledged, he is much more willing to validate a woman's feelings, thoughts, rights, wishes, and wants. By recognizing the good in his past or present, a woman motivates him to give more in the future. When a woman takes time to acknowledge the ways a man is supportive, he automatically becomes more capable of validating a woman's perspective. After all, it is that perspective that is giving him the support he seeks.

6. She Wants Reassurance and He Wants Encouragement

Men often make the mistake of assuming that a woman continues to feel his support because he did something supportive in the past. A man doesn't recognize the Venusian need to be assured again and again. A man might go overboard to make a woman feel welcome in a job, and then later completely ignore her, thinking he has already established that he is her friend and supporter. Women are much more aware of changes and seek to be assured that they have the same status and support as they had the day before. This tendency is similar to our mutual need to seek assurance that our stocks are still doing well. Since the market can change very quickly, it is comforting to know that our stocks are still in good standing. A man's reassuring attitude instills a sense of comfort and security in a woman that evokes her goodwill and trust in a man. She is able to believe in him when she is assured that he still supports her.

Women often make the mistake of talking too much about

potential problems when a man is seeking to find a solution. Often a man will suggest something, and very quickly a woman will see what could go wrong and point that out. This can be very discouraging for a man, and he mistakenly concludes that she doesn't recognize or appreciate his competence. Before expressing doubts or concerns it is best for her to first hear what he is suggesting and acknowledge the merit of his ideas. An encouraging attitude is open, trusting, and patient to see the good in something. To be encouraging a woman should not be quick to find fault or express concern. She may think she is just being helpful, but often such behavior increases his stress level. It is important for a woman to sense when her concern is necessary, otherwise it can be counterproductive. When a man feels encouraged by a woman's trust, appreciation, and acceptance, he seeks to be more reassuring by being more caring, understanding, and respectful of her wishes and needs.

How You May Be Inadvertently Losing Business

Without an understanding of our different emotional needs, both men and women offend, neglect, and turn off clients and customers. Instead of reducing their stress, we increase it. Although the work world is all about providing a functional service, it is also about people. You may do a great job for a great price, but when people don't feel their emotional needs are being met, they find someone else to do business with. People may say they want the best deal, but deep inside they want to feel good. When their emotional needs are not met, they may smile in your presence, but they don't come back. When people don't feel emotionally supported, they may feel hurt, jealous, resentful, offended, anxious, angry, and the whole gamut of human emotions. By taking the time to give the right kind of support, much of this can be avoided.

Customers may smile to be polite in your presence, but unless they feel supported they don't come back.

While women tend to have more "sensitive feelings," men tend to have more "sensitive egos," By making sure to give caring, understanding, respect, inclusion, validation, and reassurance, a man can avoid hurting a woman's feelings. By making sure to give trust, acceptance, appreciation, admiration, acknowledgment, and encouragement, a woman can make sure to stroke the "male ego." This not only creates more business, but creates a better business environment. When coworkers and management are more supportive, this affects customers and clients as well. When a woman client hears or sees a man being disrespectful of a woman coworker, she will often take it personally. Likewise, when a man sees women in business supporting the men, he wants to do business there.

You may have the best product, but if others don't feel emotionally supported they will go elsewhere. It is not enough to have a product you have to motivate others to test it and use it. Then they need to be motivated to tell others about it. You will go nowhere unless your customers and clients feel the emotional support they appreciate most.

The following is a list of common communication mistakes women make in relation to a man's primary emotional needs. These mistakes are most obvious with customers and clients, but the same principles apply with coworkers and management.

Mistakes women commonly make:	Why a man doesn't feel supported:
She corrects him or gives unsolicited advice. "That is not the way you are supposed to use this."	**Men want trust:** Even if she is right, he feels unsupported because he was not asking for her advice. He doesn't feel his competence is trusted.

Mistakes women commonly make:	Why a man doesn't feel supported:
She expresses impatience or frustration in the tone of her voice. "We were planning to get that done, but it wasn't our first priority."	**Men want acceptance:** He hears that he is a problem for her, when she is supposed to be supporting him. He doesn't feel accepted.
She excuses herself with a tone of being overwhelmed in her voice. "This is such a crazy season. We are way understaffed."	**Men want appreciation:** He hears that she is burdened by his business and he doesn't feel appreciated.
She offers her assistance when he has not asked. " Let me help you with that . . ."	**Men want admiration:** A man doesn't feel admired when he is perceived to be needing help when that help is not necessary.
She defends a mistake by blaming something or someone else without taking time to acknowledge what the client did to make his need clear. "Where is my staff when I need them . . . ?"	**Men want acknowledgment:** He hears that she is not being accountable. He doesn't feel that he is being clearly acknowledged for doing what was required of him.
She complains about her company and their policies. "I can't get them to change this."	**Men want encouragement:** He hears her frustration with her company and is not encouraged to do business with her company.

In each of these examples it becomes clear how a woman might say or do something that on her planet is supportive but is not on Mars. Men make the same kind of mistakes. They give the support a man might want, but not what women recognize as support. The following is a list of communication mistakes men make in relation to a woman's primary emotional needs.

Mistakes men make:

He listens briefly and then offers a solution right away. "I think you should . . ."

He doesn't ask questions to learn more about her problem or request but responds with a sense of confidence that the problem can be easily solved. "No problem, we can handle that."

He expresses a company policy with a tone of acceptance and surrender. "There is nothing more I can do, rules are rules."

A man will often listen to a woman's ideas, proposals, and requests without displaying any movement, response, or emotion.

When a woman is dissatisfied, a man will seek to offer something else as a way to compensate for her loss. "Try this option instead. It will work just as well."

Why she doesn't feel supported:

Women want consideration: A woman doesn't feel as if he cares to hear everything she is thinking or what she thinks she should do. His inconsiderate attitude is a turnoff to her.

Women want understanding: She feels as if he is making light of a problem. By minimizing the problem he makes her feel minimized or dismissed. A woman would be frustrated that he doesn't understand the whole problem.

Women want respect: A woman hears his statement as indifference to her need and feels disrespected. She would prefer something like, "I am so sorry that I cannot . . ."

Women want inclusion: A woman will feel his poker face is a sign that he is either uninterested or he is hiding something. She then feels excluded or on the outside.

Women want validation: A woman will not feel supported because her need to feel validated has not been met. She wants him to take more time to recognize her loss.

Mistakes men make:	Why she doesn't feel supported:
When a man does not have anything good to report, he will often wait to "get back" until he either has something conclusive or he has some good news.	**Women want reassurance:** A woman will misinterpret his silence as bad news or a lack of caring on his part. Women are much quicker to get back to someone with progress reports.

In dealing with customers and clients, it is obvious that if we want to be successful, it falls on us to give as much support as we can. After all, they are paying us to serve them. In other areas of the workplace, it is equally true but not so obvious. Our work relationships at all levels are based on earning our way. The only way to earn the support you want is to give what others want. Nothing will fall in your lap unless you generate it.

How to Earn a Woman's Support

The most effective way a man can succeed in earning the support of women is with strong communication. By learning to listen a man can most effectively demonstrate an attitude that is caring, understanding, respectful, inclusive, validating, and reassuring. By communicating in this manner, he will be minimizing her stress levels and earning her support in return.

One of the biggest problems men have with listening is they forget our different styles of communicating and become frustrated or angry. The chart below outlines what he needs to remember and makes some suggestions about what to do.

How Men Can Listen Without Getting Frustrated

What to remember:

Remember, frustration comes from not understanding her point of view, and this is never her fault.

Remember, feelings don't always make sense right away, but they are still valid and deserve empathy. Even if her feelings make you feel blamed, it doesn't justify raising your voice and dumping your anger on her.

Frustration and anger often come from not knowing what to do to make things better. Remember that you are trying to make things better and getting upset only makes things worse.

Remember, you don't have to agree with her to validate her perspective. Women do not require agreement, but they do resist put-down statements like, "That's stupid" or "That's

What to do and not to do:

Be accountable for not understanding. Don't blame her for upsetting you. Remember her way of communicating is just as valid. Suck it up and start again, trying to see things from her perspective.

Take a few deep breaths with the intention to relax. Don't say anything. The worst thing to do when you are angry is to speak without calmly thinking first. When the expression of anger is resisted by another, and it will be, it is comparable to putting gas on a fire, it just makes you angrier.

Don't blame her because your solutions are not working. Listen more, and she may come up with a solution. If you involve her in the solution, she will appreciate you more.

Hold back from making demeaning comments to express your disagreement with a behavior or idea. Don't use negative adjectives or nouns to put others down. Express what

What to remember:

ridiculous." You think you are putting down a behavior, but she takes it personally.

A man can stay relaxed by remembering there is light at the end of the tunnel. As women talk without being interrupted, they automatically become more open and receptive to what a man has to say.

Remember, she is not responsible for your anger. Men get angrier when they think she is making him angry. Don't be a victim and blame her. You have lost your cool, she didn't take it. If she doesn't appreciate what you are saying, back off, listen more, and then she will appreciate you more.

Remember, you don't have to do what she is suggesting. You are still in the middle of a negotiation.

What to do and not to do:

you don't agree with and what you would appreciate instead without direct put-down statements.

When you feel pressured to interrupt and make your point, instead of saying you understand *do the opposite*. Kindly let her know that you don't understand what she is saying, and let her know you want to. Show an interest in taking more time to get what she is saying, and she will do the same for you. With this confidence, you will not succumb to counterproductive behavior, and your anger will cool down.

If you wish to offer a solution or make the situation better, make sure she is finished and rephrase her point of view to her satisfaction before giving your own. Do not raise your voice.

Don't argue with feelings and opinions when someone is emotionally upset. Take a time-

What to remember:

Her emotional tone may sound final to him, but on Venus emotions mean she is not yet final in her perspective. Negative emotions first need to be heard before they become more positive.

What to do and not to do:

out to discuss things later when there is less emotional charge. Simply say, "Let me think about this more and then let's talk about it." Don't say, "You are too upset about this for me to talk with you."

When a man can listen to a woman's feelings without getting angry or frustrated, he earns her trust, acceptance, and appreciation and minimizes her stress. When he makes it safe for her to experience an occasional rise and fall of emotions in the workplace, she is more than willing to accept his shortcomings while appreciating, acknowledging, and admiring his successes. The more a woman feels understood the more she can give back to a man the support he wants.

How to Earn a Man's Support

Women can learn to support men by doing less and receiving more. When a woman enlists the support of a man in some way, she automatically gains the ability to shower him with trust, acceptance, appreciation, admiration, acknowledgment, and encouragement.

The secret of enlisting his support is to avoid trying to change him or improve him. Certainly you may want him to change—just don't act on that desire. Only if he directly or specifically asks for advice is he open to your assistance.

This is often why many men have difficulty with female managers. When a woman feels responsible for a man's action, she may take even more liberty than a male manager to tell him what to do. Men sense when a man has received enough direction and back off from too many helpful suggestions.

A woman manager will take even more liberty to improve a man and tell him what to do.

If a man is resistant to her authority, a woman manager, thinking she is being more inclusive, will seek consensus rather than assert her authority and directly ask a man to do something the way she wants it done. She will soften her request with phrases like, "Don't you think . . . ," "Maybe it would be better to . . . ," or "Could you try it this way. . . ." This tendency to soften her power to direct his behavior is appreciated on Venus, but not on Mars. To him, her phrasing sounds like she is not sure. He reasons that it is unfair to impose her thinking when she is unsure and he is not.

Her friendly suggestions can also be offensive. If he is required to change his approach to do something her way, it is much better for her to be direct. Seeking his consensus, when her wish is backed up by her authority as manager, only creates more stress. On Mars, submitting to her "softened" request makes it appear as if he agrees that her way is better than his way. To help him save face, a male manager doesn't soften his requests but instead uses his authority by directly asking. In this way, the employee is complying because it is his job to comply, and not because his way is deficient.

A male manager will relate to the Martian's need to save face and directly ask another man to do something rather than point out he has a better way to do it. If a woman is to pull rank, she should be direct about it in a pleasant manner. Men respect hierarchy. If she is the boss, she has certain rights. When she minimizes her authority and gives helpful advice as a coworker, but then later requires compliance, he is put off. Here are a few examples:

Avoid indirectness, don't say:	Be direct and say:
It would probably work better if you talked to Sam before you put in that order.	Would you talk to Sam first before putting in the order?
Don't you think it would be best if you finished this before moving your office.	Would you finish this first before moving your office?
I am not so sure you should make that appointment. I think it is Richard's territory.	Would you talk to Richard first before making that appointment? I think it is Richard's territory.
Maybe we should let them know that we are not willing to make these changes.	Would you let them know that we are not willing to make these changes?
Could you let Tom know that I am not interested in the that program?	Please, tell Tom that I am not interested in that program.
Would you be willing to return this for me?	Would you return this for me?
Do you think, maybe, you could stop doing that?	Would you please stop doing that?

If a woman remembers to make direct requests rather than making "polite" indirect requests, a man becomes more receptive. The suggestions above are not just for managers to use with male employees, they are equally useful in dealing with male coworkers, clients, patients, and customers as well. Men always appreciate directness.

For women to recognize how these small adjustments could be so important on Mars, let's take a very Venusian example. Imagine a man on his knees, asking for a woman's hand in marriage. Instead of saying, "Would you marry me?" he says, "Could you marry me?"

Even if she is already willing to marry him, it would give her cause to think about it for a moment. Instead of inspiring and motivating her heart to open, his choice of words creates the opposite response.

So much time is wasted when men and women at all levels of the workplace unknowingly offend each other. With a greater awareness of the six primary needs of the opposite sex, you will have an extra tool to achieve your goals and earn the recognition, respect, and trust that you deserve. As men and women in the workplace support each other more effectively, emotional tension decreases while cooperation and collaboration increase; stress is minimized, and productivity goes up.

11

Standing Up and Standing Out

The work environment is in many ways the opposite of a family environment. In a nurturing family, people care for each other according to their needs. In the work environment, you may need business, but that doesn't motivate people to buy your products or use your services. Just because you need more money to pay your bills, you are not going to get a job. You may have the talent, but unless you can convince someone else, you will not be rewarded. The workplace is not a charity. You are rewarded based on the results you create. It is up to you to make sure others are aware of your skills and abilities. People may like you, but if they are not aware of your abilities you will not get the job.

Men realize this and promote themselves whenever possible. A man looks for ways to stand up higher than others and stand out from the crowd. This is opposite to the way women think. Women are more egalitarian and inclusive. Since building up one's special talents, abilities, and achievements can create a sense of division, on Venus differences are downplayed. This tendency creates a serious disadvantage for women in a workplace in which men and women with Martian tendencies are the primary decision makers.

A man looks for a way to stand up higher than others and stand out from the crowd.

By understanding the way men perceive power and competence, a woman gains a competitive edge to make sure she gets the same opportunities that a man will get. Likewise, a man gains a competitive edge by understanding how women perceive power and competence differently.

The Perception of Power

When men interact, they are always evaluating the level of competence of others. A man is always focused on the score, and the score is always changing. He measures himself by the score and so do others. Though this seems cruel and heartless, it is a fact of life. Just as women are often unfairly judged by their age and looks, men are often judged by their salary. When a woman tells her parents whom she wants to marry, one of their first questions is often "What does he do?"

Ultimately everyone deserves unconditional love, but the workplace is very conditional. If you want the job, you have to prove that you can do it. Respect on Mars always goes to whoever is winning. People naturally want to do business with the best. The bottom line in the workplace is that competence earns respect.

Yet competence is not enough. Others must be aware of your competence. It is not enough to have the best product on the market. You have to let others know that you have the best product. From this perspective marketing is everything. Power in the workplace does not only involve competence, but even more important is the perception of power. If others see you as powerful, you gain a greater power to influence others.

On Mars, the perception of power earns the greatest respect.

Men instinctively respect and follow those they perceive to have greater power. On Mars, a man's sense of self is primarily defined by his sense of competence. He prides himself in his ability to solve problems or get a job done. As his accomplishments increase, he will tend to advertise his achievements and abilities in a variety of ways, sometimes subtle and sometimes not.

On Venus competence is important, but compassion, caring, integrity, and other more personal values take precedence. As a result, women don't advertise their competence, but instead are proud of their caring, goodness, responsiveness, dedication, and willingness to serve. The infusion of these qualities into the workplace are making it a better place. Women will have greater influence in the workplace as they learn to incorporate the Martian ways of promoting competence.

On Venus competence is important, but compassion, caring, integrity, and other more personal values take precedence.

Women tend to hide the qualities and attributes that could generate respect from men in the workplace. When a woman doesn't actively promote herself, a man assumes that she doesn't have anything to promote. Unless a woman learns to stand up higher than others and stand out from the crowd, she sabotages her success with men.

In a similar way, when men build themselves up too much,

they build walls of resistance on Venus. The very attributes that make men stand out can minimize the respect and trust he gets from women. Women want to do business with someone who takes time to recognize their value and consider their needs. A man can still stand up and stand out if he balances his Martian assertiveness with an equal demonstration of Venusian values. By becoming more sensitive to how others feel in his presence, he can stand out more by creating better work relationships.

Learning to Take Credit

A woman will often minimize her accomplishments or attribute her success either to good luck or the help of others. She may feel very proud but she will not let others know. She does not realize the importance of standing up for herself and standing out by taking credit for her achievements and accomplishments. Someone might compliment her on what a great job she did, and in response, she might say, "Well, I had a lot of help."

In this example, she is downplaying her role to maintain a sense of inclusiveness and relatedness to her peers. To stand up and out, she needs to take credit for what she has done by saying something confident like, "I'm really very proud of it too. It just gets easier and easier." On Venus, this is the last thing she would do. It would appear arrogant, vain, or "too self-promoting." She could easily lose the approval of other women.

**On Venus they frown and disapprove
when a woman boasts about her accomplishments.**

It is fine to thank others when you are being awarded for your achievements, but only when it is clear that you are really the responsible one. In the workplace, by humbly minimizing her achievements, a woman creates a perception on Mars that she is not as competent as she truly is. By *only* crediting others for her achievement, she leads a man to assume that she really isn't that responsible for her accomplishments and doubt her competence. When she credits her success to good fortune, downplaying her superior talent, skill, and excellent application, a man will assume she is not really competent but just lucked out. When a woman says, "I don't deserve this recognition, it belongs to my team," a man could take her literally. A woman would see her as being gracious.

> **By *only* crediting others for her achievement, a woman leads a man to doubt her competence.**

The presentations of awards, perks, recognition, and review meetings are a great addition to the workplace. They allow women to freely stand up and stand out without the concerns that they are too full of themselves.

Occasional awards or perks are helpful, but ultimately a woman needs to develop the ability to take credit at all times. In an ideal world, people would recognize the value and benefit of others, but that is not the workplace. On the one hand, a woman needs to respect her instinctive Venusian values, but on the other hand, she needs to take credit for her achievements to demonstrate her degree of competence.

To maintain a sense of humility and acknowledge her competence, a woman can thank others, but *after* she first takes credit in some way. This enables her to feel inclusive of others but still focuses on her success. For example, she could respond to a compliment by saying, "I am really proud as well. It just gets easier and easier. But I couldn't have done it without the support of others. . . ." By acknowledging herself first, she is free to go on to acknowledge others.

In the business world, to be most supportive of others, we need to let them know what we have to offer. In a corporation,

those decision makers responsible for promotions need your help
to determine who is best for higher levels of responsibility. They
are looking to you, but if you don't take credit, someone else
will, and you will not be seen. With this insight, a woman can
feel more comfortable promoting herself. By promoting herself,
she is also supporting those whom she wishes to serve.

A Sign from Above

When I wrote *Men Are from Mars, Women Are from Venus*, I
faced this conflict within myself. I didn't feel comfortable with
infomercials, but they were an effective way to stand up and
stand out. It seemed in bad taste to have a beautiful and helpful
message and then cheapen it by "advertising" its effectiveness. It
seemed arrogant to promote the incredible benefits of my workshops. I prayed for several months about this dilemma.

Then I got my answer on a vacation with my wife, Bonnie,
and youngest daughter, Lauren. We went on a driving trip from
California to the Shakespeare Festival in Ashland, Oregon. They
were sold out for the show we wanted to see, but we were told
you could wait before the performance to buy tickets from people who were not using theirs. When I arrived thirty minutes before the performance, there were about forty people with the
same idea.

After about five minutes, someone with tickets came up. Before I even noticed, he was mobbed from all sides by people
wanting tickets. This was discouraging. I didn't want to push
ahead of others, nor did I want to mob someone. I thought
about how uncomfortable that must be for the ticket seller. I just
continued to stand there not knowing what I would do.

About five minutes later, I noticed a man buying tickets from
another person who had arrived. This man had a little piece of
paper saying, "Need two tickets for tonight's *Midsummer*

Night's Dream." He was standing away from the crowd. When a ticket seller arrived, he automatically went to him.

After their exchange the man walked away. I went and asked him for his sign. I changed the words to three tickets, stood away from the crowd, and waited. Within a few minutes I was approached by someone who wanted to avoid the crowd and sell me tickets. I bought the tickets, but they still weren't the best seats. So I waited and continued to buy more tickets until I got really good seats.

As I started buying more tickets, a small group of women stood next to me hoping to buy the tickets I didn't want. These women were so relieved and grateful to get tickets. Within ten minutes, I got better seats and sold my other tickets. It was amazing to me that as it became apparent that I was getting my pick of the best seats no one else put up a sign of their own.

When I was done, I started to walk away and still no one had asked me for my sign. I went up to one woman and offered her my sign. She was so grateful. It was amazing to me that out of this crowd of forty people no one else had caught on or felt comfortable standing up and standing out. By offering her my sign, she could then give herself permission to stand out.

Well, we had great seats for the performance, but more important for me, I had gotten what I was looking for. My prayer had been answered. I now recognized the value of an infomercial. This event had given me the permission I needed to stand out. Unless I took responsibility to let others know what I had to offer, they wouldn't know. It was my job to put up my sign and then it was up to them to pick and choose what they wanted to do.

Years later, I returned to the Shakespeare Festival with Bonnie. This time more people were using little signs to stand out. Yet to my amazement it was still only about twenty percent. There was still a hungry crowd ready to pounce on the next ticket seller, even though most ticket sellers immediately went to those who stood out by carrying signs.

Let Your Results Speak for Themselves

Another approach for staying humble while taking credit comes from Mars. A more humble man will often build up his results but not himself. He will not just say, "Yes, I did a great job again." Instead, he would say, "I did a great job. Mr. Parker was very happy with the results." By focusing on the results, he can take credit without putting anyone else down in the process.

This approach is helpful for women, but women still feel uncomfortable with the "I" word. A woman is more comfortable using "we," even when she is primarily responsible for an achievement. When a woman uses "we" instead of "I," it is very misleading to men. On Mars, they eagerly take credit for whatever they can, so when a woman is not taking credit or building up her results, men mistakenly conclude she is less competent.

**When a woman doesn't take credit,
a man assumes she is less confident and competent.**

To stand up and stand out when working with men, a woman needs to practice taking credit using the "I" word and not relying on the "we" word. It takes practice to build yourself up and take credit without sounding or feeling arrogant. In the beginning, it will be awkward and unfamiliar, but with practice it will become natural and flowing.

A woman or man will experience immediate benefits by practicing taking credit in front of a mirror before work. First write out a list of achievements big and small. Then write out how you could take credit by using the "I" word while emphasizing the result. Finally, take a few minutes to practice taking credit out loud standing straight, with chest up. You should then practice them over and over. This can be as simple as thinking about an achievement and saying out loud, "I did a good job."

Another version of this technique is to imagine others acknowledging you and saying you did a good job. Then in response say out loud, "You are right, I did a good job."

As you become more comfortable taking credit at home in private, others at work will give you more recognition. By focusing a few minutes a day on standing up and standing out, you will also begin to notice all the different ways you set yourself up to be overlooked.

In the following examples, notice in the Venus approach the emphasis is on "we." In the second column, notice with the Mars approach the emphasis is on the result. The "I" is mentioned mainly for clarification. By focusing on the result, a man conveys a certain sense of humility while standing up and standing out. What he focuses on is the result of his actions and not him. In the third column, both approaches are combined to create a Mars/Venus approach. Using this approach, women are not offended and a woman can get the recognition and credit she deserves from men. Notice in the third column often the "I" is used first and then "we."

Venus Approach: *Share credit.*	Mars Approach: *Take credit and focus on results.*	Mars/Venus approach: *Take credit, share credit and focus on results.*
We did a great job.	I am really proud of this job. It has surpassed my expectations.	I am very proud of this job, but I could not have done it without the help of my team. It has surpassed my expectations.
We all worked really hard.	I don't think I have ever worked so hard, but it was worth it. It	I worked really hard on this project and got a lot of support

Venus Approach: *Share credit.*	Mars Approach: *Take credit and focus on results.*	Mars/Venus approach: *Take credit, share credit and focus on results.*
	is really good, and many people will benefit.	from my team. It is really good and many people will benefit.
We changed our approach and now we have several branches.	I implemented a new approach, and now I have opened several branches to serve even more people.	I implemented a new approach, and now we have opened several branches to serve even more people.
We came up with a better way of doing it.	I came up with a new approach, and now I am getting much better results. Everyone is pleased.	I came up with a new approach and now we are getting much better results. Everyone is pleased.
Henry agreed, and now we have the deal.	I called Henry and closed the deal. Now there will be no more delays, and everyone can move forward.	I called Henry, and we closed the deal. Now there will be no more delays, and we can all move forward.
The project is finally finished, and we did a great job.	I spent the last three weeks finishing up, and now it looks great. It will be smooth sailing from here on.	I spent the last three weeks finishing up, and now it looks great. We did a great job. It will be smooth sailing from here on.

Venus Approach: *Share credit.*	Mars Approach: *Take credit and focus on results.*	Mars/Venus approach: *Take credit, share credit and focus on results.*
We implemented a new approach in San Diego, and sales have doubled.	Since I implemented this new approach on my trip to San Diego, I have doubled sales. Everyone can now use this new approach.	Since I implemented this new approach, we have doubled sales. Everyone can now use this new approach.
By waiting a week, we got a much better deal.	By holding back for a week, I got a much better deal. Now our profits will go up.	By holding back for a week, we got a much better deal. Now our profits will go up.

Another activity is to make a list for another whom you admire or with whom you work with. Make a list of his or her achievements. Pretend to be that person and take credit. Sometimes it is easier to give others permission to take credit than to give it to ourselves. By role-playing, being someone else in the mirror, you can begin to feel that it is okay.

Your friends want you to take credit for your success, and if they don't, they aren't your friends anyway. The bottom line in business is that your customers, clients, and managers clearly want you to take credit. To be considerate toward them, it behooves you to stand up and stand out.

Keeping Score on Mars

Men readily let others know their accomplishments in the same way that they keep track of the score in a sporting event. On

Mars, stating the score is not an ego trip, but instead a way of letting others know a Martian's competence.

By building himself up, he is not arrogantly putting others down. He is merely letting others know the facts so that they will be assured he can be trusted for the job. On Mars, humility has more to do with not putting others down to put yourself up. It is just healthy self-esteem to put yourself forward if your results back you up. Instead of putting others down, a Martian uses the list of his achievements to build himself up. On his planet, this is a sign of humility.

**On Mars, humility has to do with
not putting others down to put yourself up.**

When a project is completed, often it is not clear who is most responsible for the success. After all, many people are often involved. Women mistakenly assume that if they work hard others will notice their achievements and point them out. Because she wants to appear humble, she will not assert herself to get more credit. A woman doesn't realize that if she doesn't take credit, then someone else will get the credit that she deserves. Unless she participates in pointing out her score, she will be overlooked.

**Women make the mistake of assuming
that if they work hard, then others will notice
their achievements and give them credit.**

In the movie business, it used to be that actors were overlooked. The studios tried to keep all the credit. Gradually, movie stars became more important than the houses. Movie directors and writers were still overlooked. Then movie directors started using new unknown actors to make great films. When the actors didn't automatically get the attention, then these directors could claim it. Scriptwriters are still basically overlooked. A few are now starting to get more attention and credit. Ultimately, she or he who gets credit is that person who successfully claims credit and then markets his or her success so others know about it.

When an actor or actress gets top billing, the credit wasn't just given because someone thought the star deserved it. Through their agents and managers, they negotiated for that top credit. Getting credit is often a battle that is best fought before the event and not after. That is the point of contracts. On Mars you get the credit you negotiated. Fair is what you negotiate. Your power to negotiate is based on credit for past successes.

On Mars, fair is what you negotiate.

Self-promotion is the basis of all the TV awards programs. By publicly giving awards, different areas of the entertainment industry have a chance to sing their own glories. Movie attendance automatically goes up after the Academy Awards are aired. Shortly thereafter the price of movie tickets goes up another fifty cents.

TV is now filled with awards programs. The Oscars, Grammy Awards, Golden Globes, Emmys, MTV, and VH1 Music Awards, Peoples Choice Awards, etc., are all effective ways for the entertainment industry to stand up and stand out. By recognizing leaders in their industry, they increase awareness and attention from the public. Suddenly people are supporting their business more.

In the workplace, the perception of success generates more success. As women take more time to promote themselves, others will perceive them as being more powerful and their competence will then be recognized.

Wise women and men send reports to their bosses and managers and let them see positive correspondence from coworkers or with clients. They make sure that they get a chance to report the ideas and suggestions they generated. They take time to network with others at lunch and social functions. They fill their office with awards, certificates, pictures of loved ones, pictures linking them with an achievement, and pictures of them associated with well-known people. A picture is worth a thousand words of support without you having to say anything.

Humor on Mars and Venus

The male tendency to put himself up and a woman's tendency to put herself down shows up in a variety of places in the workplace, from small talk during a break to casual jokes and comments throughout the day. It is particularly evident in our preference in humor. What is often funny to a man is not funny to a woman, and when a woman thinks she is being funny, a man may not realize she made a joke. On Venus, women often mock themselves in self-effacing ways to lighten things up, but a man takes it literally. On Mars, humor involves mocking others in demeaning or threatening ways often using profanities. Women don't like it because they take it literally.

Humor on Mars and Venus is very different. Men tend to put others down, but women tend to put themselves down. Male humor makes men appear intimidating to women. Female humor makes women appear incompetent to men. Both men and women can score big with the opposite sex when they laugh at their jokes or at least have an accepting attitude that doesn't disapprove.

If a woman does not really appreciate a man's humor, she can let it be known without putting him down. If he has made a joke, he needs to save face. In a friendly way, she could simply chuckle and say something nondisapproving like, "You guys are from Mars." If she is light about it, doesn't take offense, or feel excluded, he will not exclude her. Often men laugh at other men's jokes, but don't really find them funny at all. They laugh a little as a way to save face and be supportive.

Never ask a man to explain his joke. If she doesn't get it, he will not hold it against her. Here are a few examples of what not to say and what she could say.

Responding to Male Humor

Do not say in a serious tone:	Good to say in a playful tone:
Why is that funny?	I don't get it.
I don't find that funny.	Come on, stop.
I am offended by your humor.	Hey, cut it out.
That is not funny!	Can we change the subject?
I don't appreciate your jokes!	Hey, back off.
I can't believe you would say that!	You're just kidding, right?

Ultimately, it is the playful tone that works. You could actually go down the first list, and if you used a playful tone with an accepting attitude, a man would be fine, and you would be making a good joke. The secret here is to find a voice inside that is not being hurt or taking offense by his jokes and mocking. With this playful and positive approach he will back off not because he is offending you but because he gets the idea that you are not particularly appreciative of male humor. Remember, on Mars, to take offense is to offend.

By being accepting and not disapproving of male humor, a woman scores extra points with a man. Yet for some women it is just uncomfortable. If you really want him to stop, the key is to be light about it but don't allow it. Pick a time when no one else is around and directly ask him to stop.

Here is an example: "Do me a favor, would you stop making jokes around me. I know some people find them really funny but

I don't. Thanks." Don't wait for a reply, just assume that he will do his best and in a friendly way walk away. The less you say or he says, the better. This gives him a chance to grumble inside and eventually change his behavior. If he gets into a big discussion and defends his humor, then it will be harder for him to respond to her request.

If he persists, the best key for you is to ignore it and not let it get to you. It may be that sometimes he just forgets. By ignoring it, or playfully rolling your eyes, he will stop. You shouldn't be too playful, or he will be encouraged to continue this playful exchange.

When Women Use Male Humor

Men playfully banter back and forth challenging each other's competence in a tone that says, "Just kidding." One man might say, "You can't do that, you are a loser." And his friend will say back, "I can too. You don't even have a clue about what's going on."

For a woman to join into this kind of playful dialog, she has to take everything lightly, and not be offended by anything. If she were to take offense at a man's banter and say back, "I can too! You don't even have a clue . . ." she could be starting an argument.

A woman could use the very same words a man would use to make a joke and end up insulting a man. It is not her words that offend, but the tone of her voice or attitude. If she is resentful in any way toward a man, or men in general, she runs the risk of offending.

Sarah, a ticket agent, made a joking comment about Larry, a male coworker. She said, "Men, they never know what they are doing." It hit a flat note, and later she was privately reprimanded by her male boss. She felt that other men made demeaning joking comments about men. Why couldn't she? The problem was, she believed what she was saying, and the men could pick it up in her tone of voice.

If Larry had been annoyed with her about some other issue, this joke would have made it worse. Men can lighten up a situation by making jokes about another man, but a woman can't. To understand this distinction let's explore a similar situation.

A Jewish comedian can make jokes about Jews because he is Jewish, but a non-Jew cannot. It is just not acceptable and is in bad taste. Likewise, a man making jokes about men is acceptable by men, because he is a man. A woman doing it is a different matter.

**A man making jokes about men is acceptable
because he is a man.**

When a man puts men down in a humorous way, he is not excluding himself from the equation. If a woman belittles a man, because she is not a man she is not including herself. Even if she uses the same words, she alienates herself and appears as if she is saying she is better. If she were to use put-down humor regarding other women, male workers would get the humor, but other women would not appreciate it.

Just as women need to be careful in using male humor with men, men need to recognize that women often do not appreciate it. Making a joke by putting someone down is just not funny on Venus. To stand out in a positive manner, women should avoid using male humor with men unless it seems easy to do and she gets a positive result. Likewise, if men want to be respected by women, they should avoid using male humor around women unless it is very clear that they appreciate it.

Understanding Female Humor

Female humor is self-effacing. On Venus, it is not funny to put others down; a woman can, however, put herself down. By putting herself down in some playful manner, rapport is strengthened because other women don't feel she considers herself better. Women commonly put themselves down, and though women will laugh men will take it seriously.

A man doesn't realize that a woman is just joking and takes her literally. In one moment his view of her can shift. She suddenly seems much less competent than in the previous moment. Just as a man can suddenly seem uncaring by making a put-down joke, a woman suddenly appears to a man as incompetent by putting herself down.

On Venus, self-effacing humor is just a playful way for women to exaggerate their feelings to release some stress and connect. Often a woman will do this through telling a story from her life. She will talk in great detail about a problem she was unable to solve. All the women will laugh and share similar mishaps.

With this insight, men can recognize that when women put themselves down they are not to be taken literally. Women can recognize that unless a man understands Venusian humor, he will think she is advertising her incompetence.

When a man uses female humor and puts himself down, he may be in for a surprise. Instead of laughing along with him, a woman may nod her head and agree with him. If she has any unresolved feelings of resentment or frustration, they will automatically be triggered and suddenly the whole air changes. She may remember times when he made mistakes and didn't apologize. If he playfully comments, "I completely forgot what I was supposed to say," instead of getting a warm and friendly response, he may get a stern look, saying, "Yeah, you do that."

These are some examples of how male and female humor differ. With a greater awareness of how we may sound to the opposite sex, we can make wiser choices to determine how we stand up and stand out by using humor.

Male humor:	Female humor:
You are really stupid.	I was so stupid.
Oh, grow up.	I can't believe I did that.
You can't do that.	There is no way I will ever be able to do all that.
You are lost in space.	I was so embarrassed. I had no idea what to say.
Duhh!	I completely forgot what I was supposed to do.
You are full of it.	I completely messed up.
You're out of your league.	I looked like an idiot.
You don't know what you are talking about.	Nobody had any idea of what I was talking about.
I don't believe you.	I went on and on talking, and completely forgot to ask about her daughter.
Oh, Mr. Know-It-All speaks.	I was so scared, I could have wet my pants.
So who appointed you the leader?	I was completely lost. We arrived two hours late.
I hate you.	They hated me. I was a complete disappointment.

He's Got the Scoop and She's Got the Buzz

Men often seek to stand out by knowing what is going on in the outer world, while women seek to stand out by knowing what is going on in the inner world. When men connect with small talk they often talk about sports, business, weather, and the news. A man or woman gains greater respect and recognition with men by being well informed on current events.

By only talking about the news a man misses an opportunity to strengthen his connection with a female coworker. By not sharing some details about his personal life or asking her more personal questions, she may feel as though he doesn't personally care about her. Just as a man doesn't want to miss out on the latest baseball scores, a woman doesn't want to miss out on hearing the details about one's personal life or share about herself.

**A man scores big points when he shares
some details about his personal life.**

Women are generally aware of the buzz. They stay up with what is going on in the personal lives of those they care about. Sharing and keeping personal secrets builds greater rapport among women. Small talk with women about personal issues strengthens work relationships.

When men hear women talking about personal issues they often assume women are wasting time and spreading negativity. Talking about the personal details of his life or of the company becomes a threat to his success. To a man, a woman gossiping not only makes her appear inefficient but can also make her a threat.

When men hear women talking about personal issues in the workplace they consider it wasting time or undermining the success of the company. On Venus, it may be a harmless discussion of personal details to release tension and share empathy, but on Mars it sounds like she is giving his competitors and enemies more information to attack or use against him. On Mars, the failures, weaknesses, and character flaws of a coworker or manager should be kept private. In a competitive work world this information can be used against someone.

By discussing the failures and weaknesses of coworkers a man or woman can be considered a threat.

In the workplace on Mars, men don't want to know your personal problems, nor do they want you to know theirs. A professional is there to serve others. When you bring your personal life into the equation, you are no longer completely serving the client. Now, they have to consider your needs. They don't want that. They want a clean business relationship with no strings. You pay for what you get, and you can always expect to get it.

Professionals are able to do their job regardless of how they feel that day.

If women did not have the opportunity to get their personal needs met outside the workplace, being professional would make a woman feel like she was wearing a straightjacket. Some women do feel this way because they don't take time to create a personal life outside the office to nurture their emotional needs.

Small talk is certainly helpful to reduce tension for both men and women, but too much of it in the workplace will alienate the opposite sex. To make the right impression and stand up and stand out as competent it is best to choose wisely when and how much you indulge in small talk.

How to Ask Questions and Save Face

A woman can unknowingly generate resistance in the workplace by the manner in which she asks for help. A woman, at any level of the workplace, may seek to be inclusive by asking a man what he thinks about a particular problem. He mistakenly concludes she is looking to him to solve her problem. He doesn't recognize that she is primarily asking for his help to create a sense of inclusion and connection. She doesn't want him to solve her problem, but she is looking for his participation in the problem-solving process.

In this situation, because he misunderstands her intention, if she doesn't agree with or follow his advice, he may become resentful that she wasted his time. A female manager may think she is creating team spirit and a sense of collaboration by asking a male employee what he thinks, but then it backfires and he doesn't feel supported at all. His feelings may sound like this:

> If you want my advice, don't turn around and tell me what's wrong with it. First, you don't have the answer and you come to me, and then you presume to know what is wrong with my answer. Not only do you waste my time but you go on to spend more time telling me in great detail why you don't like my answer. Since you think you know more than me, don't bother asking me for help in the first place.

This kind of Martian clearly doesn't know or appreciate the value of inclusion or collaboration. After experiencing this kind of reaction a few times, women become frustrated and perplexed with men. A woman concludes she only has two choices: do what he suggests and save a work relationship, or do what she wants and explain to him why she didn't choose his advice. The first choice doesn't work for her and the second choice doesn't work for him. From her perspective, asking for assistance and support is a "no win" proposal.

There is another choice. She can learn how to assist a man in saving face. If she does not agree with his advice, to help him save face she can make a simple comment to appreciate his advice and avoid a big discussion. Going into detail regarding why she is not going to use his ideas is most unpleasant for him.

Going into detail regarding why she is not going to use his ideas is most unpleasant for a Martian.

In some cases all she needs to say is, "That's a good idea, thanks." In other situations where she seemed to indicate that she was dependent on his help, she may need to make it more clear that she is not going to use his idea. She could say, "That makes sense. It helps me a lot in figuring out what I need to do."

This approach lets him know that she appreciates his assistance and is still in the process of determining an answer. In this way, he doesn't set himself up too high, to then take a fall when she doesn't do what he suggested.

The art of saving face is instinctive between men but women often don't understand it.

When you ask a man for a solution, he feels very complimented. He assumes that you don't have an answer and you have come to him because you consider him an expert. With a certain pride, he puts on his Mr. Fix-It hat and gives a solution. After he gives his answer, a woman has two choices. The first is she likes his answer and responds with appreciation. The second is she doesn't like the answer or doesn't plan to use it.

In this second case, another man will assist Mr. Fix-It in saving face. He will avoid getting into a big discussion about why he is not going to use his suggestion. Instead, he will make a casual comment like, "That's a good idea, thanks." With this face-saving comment, he lets Mr. Fix-It know that his time is appreciated, even though he may not be using his idea. The fact that he is not going to use the idea is implied, but not directly stated.

Often, before asking for help, a man will indicate by the tone of voice and attitude that he is just looking for some assistance. He might say, "I have talked to several other experts and I wondered what you thought." In this manner he doesn't set Mr. Fix-It up too high in case his advice is not followed.

In a variety of ways, a man seeking help will give the impression that he basically knows what to do but needs a little help or another perspective before he decides what to do. He might say, "Let me bounce some ideas off you. In this situation what would *you* do?"

Unless a man is ready to try what is suggested, he will not say, "What do you think *I* should do?" Women are not aware of this. By asking for his suggestions and then not following his directions, a woman unknowingly sets a man up to be frustrated.

To be precise, a man is not frustrated that she doesn't do what he says. His frustration comes from being set up as an expert and then not being treated like one. If you paid an expert to fly across the country to visit your company, and paid him ten times what everyone else made, you would at least try what he suggested before assuming to know better. You would not presume to know more. Usually a man doesn't demand that you treat him as a special expert, but if you set him up as one, he will feel annoyed when he is not treated like one.

To avoid this friction, a woman doesn't have to do whatever a man suggests. She must be careful to not set him up by putting herself way down. When she says, "I don't know what to do," it is an even bigger insult if she then corrects what he thinks. From his perspective, if she first puts herself low on the scale of expertise regarding a problem, she then puts him below her by rejecting his advice or correcting him.

In reviewing the following chart, it becomes clear how insulting a woman's comments could be when she responds to his advice by disagreeing or appearing to know more than he. In column one we will explore what not to say. In the second column, a woman can make a small change so that she doesn't set him up for the fall. In the third column are suggested ways she could allow him to save face if she doesn't plan to use his advice.

What not to say:	A better way to ask for help:	A way to help save face when you disagree:
I have no idea what to do. What do you think I should do?	This is a tough problem. What would you do?	Thanks, I feel more relieved. This was really helpful for me to figure out what I should do.
I just can't figure out what we should do. What do you think I should do?	I think I am missing something here. How would you approach this?	Thanks, that makes sense. I think I am now one big step closer to figuring out my solution.
I am so glad you are here, I really need your help. What do you think we should do?	I'm so glad you are here. What would you do in this situation?	Thanks for your support. I think now I will be able to make a better decision.
I am completely lost, what do you think I should do?	I'm taking too much time with this. What would you do if . . . ?	Thanks, another perspective really helps stimulate some new ideas to solve this problem.

What not to say:	A better way to ask for help:	A way to help save face when you disagree:
I just don't know what we should do, would you help?	I am still not getting this problem. From your perspective, what would you do?	That's a good idea. I think I now have a much better idea of the direction I want to take.
I am so confused. What do you think I should do?	I am still in the process of figuring out this problem. What would you do?	Great suggestion. I think now I am more prepared to decide what I am going to do.
This is way over my head. What do you think I should do?	I am looking for other perspectives. How would you approach this problem?	Thanks, I would have never thought of that. It is really helpful to have a different point of view.

Through periodically reviewing the different insights in this chapter both men and women can make sure they are standing up and standing out to make the right impression. A greater understanding of the different ways men and women interpret each other gives you the ability and encouragement to express yourself with confidence. Knowing how people will respond to you allows you to pick and choose how to best express yourself to achieve your personal goals in the workplace.

12

Scoring Points in the Workplace

A man scores big in the workplace when he does something that demonstrates his competence and skill. When he asserts himself and succeeds, he gets more points, but if he fails, he loses points. When he closes a deal, develops a successful plan, achieves a goal, earns money, finishes a project, or overcomes a challenge, he gets points according to how big a goal it was, how much money he made, or how big a challenge he overcame. If it is a little achievement he gets fewer points. If it is a little failure, he loses fewer points. In this manner, men measure themselves and others by their competence and achievements.

On Venus, women score points differently. A woman scores big by doing things that demonstrate her caring, consideration, and dedication. Success is not measured by how big a supportive gesture is but by consistency. It is not size that counts, but how much personal consideration is given. On Venus, they get points for trying. It is not the result that counts but the thought, consideration, or intention behind an action. On Venus, competence and achievement are not the main objectives.

**On Venus the quality of their work relationships
determines the respect and admiration women give.**

For a man to succeed in dealing with women he needs to take into consideration the way women score points differently. Women give only one point for each consideration no matter how big or small. In practical terms, this means by doing a lot of little things a man will score more than if he was to do one big thing. It does not matter how big a result he creates. It is just one point. If he ignores the work relationship, he may easily lose the opportunity to score ten points.

**Women give only one point for each expression of
consideration no matter how big or small.**

It is very common in the workplace for a male manager to come in to make a company more efficient and completely offend all the women. Soon the women are either leaving the company or refusing to work with the man. Though he may be making the company more efficient, by not scoring points with the women he will create increasing tension, which limits productivity as well as job satisfaction. When men are working with women, they can be much more effective by remembering to acquire points by building a considerate and respectful work relationship.

In sales, when dealing with women, it is clearly the quality of the relationship that counts. Let's look at an example:

Larry is a sales rep for health products. His products were good, but other reps carried similar products. When he met Jackie, who was the buyer for the center, he focused on establishing a good working relationship instead of rushing to push the benefits of his products over other products. He was upbeat, positive, interested in her experiences, and not pushy. He asked questions and got to know her a little bit. Each time he nodded his head or related to her in some way he was actually scoring points.

Jackie wasn't that interested in getting new products, but she did appreciate his interest in her needs and experiences with her products instead of trying to push his own. During their conversation, she had asked a question for which he didn't have an answer. The next day he left a message for her with the answer. When he returned the next time, rather than getting right to the point, he made small talk and asked a few questions. He asked about her kids and whether they had a good vacation. He had also noticed that Jackie's hair had changed. He simply said, "I noticed you've changed your hair. It looks good." Each of these little details scored points with Jackie.

Now Jackie makes a point of seeing him when he comes. After a few more visits, she started to order more of his products. Jackie preferred him over other sales reps because together they had built a caring and trusting work relationship. Even when she is really busy, she will take time out to see him when he comes around.

When a man doesn't understand the importance of small talk or small gestures of support, he will focus on what he can do for a woman to solve her problem or provide the best product at the best deal. This kind of support is important to her, but it only scores one point. In other words, calling her back the next day gets as many points as having a great answer to her question. Asking a question and remembering the name of her children gets as many points as saving her twenty percent on an order. By focusing his attention on doing "the little things to demonstrate caring and consideration," a man can score big with a woman.

Scoring Points on Venus

There are a variety of ways a man can score points with women in the workplace without having to do more than they are already doing. It is just a matter of redirecting the attention and energy he is already giving. Most men already know about many of these things but just don't bother to do them because they don't score that many points on Mars. When a man realizes how important they are on Venus, he is more motivated to do them. They are actually quite easy. What man doesn't enjoy getting points for doing something easy?

Understanding this one point is like discovering a treasure box in your backyard. Without having to do more, a man can make a much bigger difference in the workplace. By focusing on the little things, a man can have a much greater impact in the workplace.

> **By doing more of the little things,**
> **a man has a bigger impact in the workplace.**

One way to understand a woman's need for reassurance by scoring lots of points with small gestures is to compare this need to a car's requirement for gas. A car needs gas to drive. You may fill up the tank, but it gets used up and needs to be filled again. In a similar manner, a woman's emotional support tank gets filled up, but gets consumed. Her tank becomes empty by doing lots of little things for others. When a man does little things that say she is considered, understood, respected, validated, and included, her tank is filled again, and she is reassured that she is and will be supported. Rather than resist this difference a wise man learns to do what she requires and enjoys the benefits of getting what he wants.

What follows is a list of 101 little ways a man can top off a woman's emotional tank. This is not a list of rules a man should follow or do every day, but a checklist of little things he may be forgetting to do to remind him to include them when and where they may seem appropriate. Most of these gestures would also score points with men too. The difference is that to men they don't matter as much as getting the job done.

101 Ways to Score Points with a Woman

1. Give a personal greeting and use her name when arriving at the office instead of first asking a business question.
2. Ask a woman about her family or personal life. "How was your weekend trip?"
3. Notice when she is looking particularly good and acknowledge it with a nonsexual compliment.
4. Be aware of changes in her office and environment and comment on them.
5. Use her name when talking to her and remember the names of her spouse or boyfriend and children.
6. Recognize that women are often more sensitive to their working environment and do something to make it more pleasant. Bring fresh flowers for the office.
7. Offer to assist her whenever she is moving something heavy.
8. Notice when she seems stressed or overwhelmed and offer an empathetic comment like, "There is so much to do" or "What a day this is."
9. Notice when she gets her hair cut and make a comment that she looks really good.

10. Give more compliments regarding her work.

11. Ask specific questions about her day that indicate an awareness of what she is working on.

12. Send her an e-mail or newspaper clipping related to what she is working on or an interest she has.

13. Notice when she seems tired and offer to get her a glass of water or kindly recommend that she take a break. Women like for others to notice when they are tired or overworked.

14. Use open-ended questions. Instead of saying, "Did you finish that project?" say, "How are you doing with that project?"

15. Notice when you are talking more and practice listening longer and asking more questions before making a comment in response to what she is saying.

16. When she puts herself down or minimizes her achievement, immediately build her up and give her credit for what she does.

17. Resist the temptation to solve her problems; instead try being more empathetic and ask what she is planning to do. Don't presume that she is wanting your advice.

18. Have occasional private meetings to give and receive feedback. Whether you are a manager, coworker, or employee make sure to ask, "How can I be more helpful?" and then try listening more and not explaining yourself. Give her time to get it out.

19. When a woman is talking, be careful to not look at your watch. If you really need to, be very discreet. If you need to end the conversation, be up-front rather than give subtle messages. You could say, "Excuse me, I am late to an appointment. Let's finish this later."

20. Surprise her by doing something supportive that she wasn't expecting. Women really appreciate a little support at times when they are not expecting it. For example, bring in some

extra paper for her printer even though it wasn't your job and she had not asked.

21. After a vacation, bring a little present back to her or send a postcard to the office. This makes her feel included in your life.

22. Bring pictures from a special occasion in your life to show her. It could be from a vacation or your child's achievement.

23. Show interest in her children's talents and school activities. See her child's performance in a play or attend a sporting event that the child is participating in.

24. Invite her to participate at special events in your life or your children's life.

25. Invite her to your home for a dinner with your wife.

26. Include her in group discussion conversations. Draw her out by asking her what she thinks or would like to suggest.

27. Call to let her know if you are late for an appointment.

28. If she is visiting from another town, make sure to make recommendations for places of interest to visit or good restaurants. If she doesn't ask for assistance, don't assume she would not appreciate it.

29. Use superlatives to compliment her personally or her work. Instead of "Good job," say, "This is a really great job."

30. In responding to her request, instead of saying "no problem," try saying, "It's my pleasure." This personal touch implies caring and consideration.

31. Let her know in advance when you are planning to be absent. This will help her plan to get extra help if she needs it. When a man takes time to prepare a woman for a change, she will feel he is extra considerate.

32. When doing a job, let her know you will clean up afterwards and then make sure you do.

33. When changing plans, include her in the decision-making process so she does not feel left out of the loop.

34. When a man is in the cave, recognize that a woman may feel excluded or rejected. With this awareness try to be more friendly and remember to say hello and good-bye.

35. In a workplace where roles are clearly defined, occasionally offer to do one of her little jobs. When she seems tired or overwhelmed, this is the time to let her know she is not alone.

36. When she makes a request that can be done in a few minutes, do it right away. Even if it is not urgent or important, she will feel you are making her important.

37. When she is working through lunch, offer to pick up a salad or sandwich.

38. Invite her to have lunch with you or the group you hang out with.

39. In casual settings, compliment her on how she looks, but in formal settings when men are being introduced by their credentials and accomplishments, don't mention her charm or good looks. Stick to introducing her by her credentials and work achievements.

40. Be light and self-deprecating about your own mistakes. Make sure your humor is not sexual in content or demeaning of her or others.

41. When she makes mistakes, make a reassuring gesture. She says, "I don't think I will ever finish now." He says, "You'll get it done."

42. Validate her feelings when she is upset. She says, "This is just too hard." He says, "It has been a long day." Don't say, "That is why they call it work."

43. Notice when she is tired, busy, or overwhelmed and offer to come back at another time. "I can see this isn't a good time. I'll give you a call and we can meet later."

44. Try to create time buffers so if unexpected challenges arise,

there is enough time to deal with problems and she doesn't feel more pressured.

45. When a woman asks for help, realize that asking for help is difficult on their planet. She has probably been wanting to ask for a long time. If possible, say "sure" without testing to see if she really needs it.

46. When a woman complains, don't interrupt. Before responding or explaining anything, rephrase what she is saying in a positive voice: "So you are saying that . . ." By doing this in a positive tone, she is assured that he is trustworthy and that she has been heard.

47. When you are planning to leave, let her know. Women get a little uncomfortable when men just disappear.

48. When you get a glass of water or coffee, offer to get one for her.

49. When a woman talks, turn your body to face her and don't try doing anything else at the same time. Avoid looking up or around when she is talking.

50. Make eye contact while she talks or when you shake her hand. Don't stare in her eyes but gaze in the direction of her face. Men often look away and lose the opportunity for an easy point.

51. Ask a woman what she still has to do. Women often feel relief just telling someone what they have to do. It helps them to organize their thoughts and it minimizes stress. He should refrain from telling her what she should do. If there is something that he could easily do to help, he can say so, but only after she is done talking.

52. When a man is leaving the office to make a delivery or pick up something, he could ask her if there is something he could get for her. This generates a sense of cooperation and sharing.

53. Be aware of her health. If she was sick, make sure to ask how she is feeling. If you know she is out sick, you could call to see how she is doing and suggest a health tip like, Make sure you drink lots of water.

54. Don't burden her with your personal problems, even though women like sharing the intimate details. Once you have shared your problems, she may start to worry for you.

55. Don't put her in an awkward position by putting down one of her friends in her presence or telling her secrets that she can't tell one of her friends.

56. Don't ask for too much more. Although she may seem agreeable, women often resent being expected to do more.

57. Women are much more aware of how a person dresses. Although they are more forgiving in the way a man dresses, to make the best impression in a meeting, dress up a bit and she will appreciate that you considered her important enough for you to dress up.

58. Acknowledge her achievements in the presence of others.

59. If she acknowledges you then you should in some way acknowledge her back.

60. Be considerate and consistent in some manner. For example, always recommend a good movie to see, always open the door, always e-mail an interesting article, bring a healthy treat for workers every Tuesday, or always leave the office sink completely clean when you use it. Create a personal trademark that symbolizes your consideration of others.

61. Be flexible when a woman needs to take more time talking about something. Remember the bigger picture: if she feels heard and personally supported she will be more supportive of you.

62. In a long meeting, when on the road or on location, make a point of taking regular bathroom breaks without directly implying she might need to go.

63. Be flexible in scheduling so that family emergencies can be handled. Whenever possible support a balance of family time and work time.

64. Be polite when asking for things by using the phrase "Would you" or "Would you, please," and always remember to say, "Thank you."

65. When she is on a business trip, have the hotel leave a welcoming message for her, a fruit basket, or some flowers.

66. Remember her birthday and get her a card, take her to lunch, or give her a small present.

67. On business trips or journeys, offer to drive, but don't assume that she will want you to. If she wants to drive, don't resist.

68. When you are driving be extra considerate of what makes her comfortable. A man might freely tell another man to slow down, but a woman may hold back from appearing overly sensitive. If you are a considerate driver, she can trust you will be considerate in other dealings with her.

69. When you get angry, stop talking, take a few deep breaths, and drink a glass of water. She will be aware that you are holding back your anger and will appreciate it.

70. Notice how she is feeling and comment on it—"You look happy today" or "You look a little tired"—and then ask a question like, "What's up?" or "What is going on?"

71. When lost, stop and get directions.

72. If you say you will do something, make sure you do it. After a meeting, send a memo saying the things you agreed to do.

73. If you leave written messages for her, write clearly so she doesn't have to struggle to figure out what you are saying. A very neat note is greatly appreciated.

74. Stand up from your seat to greet her and shake her hand.

75. Always introduce her when others enter a conversation.

76. Introduce her by name and title. In glowing terms, reveal her particular participation or contribution to the company or project.

77. Show interest and reciprocate if she initiates small talk.

78. During work talk or small talk, in person or on the phone, demonstrate your interest by making little noises like ah-ha, uh-huh, oh, mmhuh, and hmmm.

79. In a group meeting, take time to point out or acknowledge the value of her contribution.

80. Give her credit where credit is due. If she gives others credit, stand up for her and let others know her contribution.

81. If she has pictures of her family on her desk ask about them.

82. If she sneezes, say, "Bless you."

83. If she spills something, quickly get up and get a towel to help clean up the mess.

84. If she has a cold, offer her some Kleenex or hot tea.

85. When an argument becomes emotionally charged, take a break gracefully. Say something like, "Give me some time to think about this, and then let's talk again."

86. Laugh or at least chuckle at her jokes instead of staring off into space or thinking about something else.

87. Before changing the subject, make sure she is finished. You could say, "If you are finished, I would like to talk about . . ."

88. Notice when she comes into the room and acknowledge her presence in some manner so she doesn't feel overlooked or ignored. If she is upset about something, ask her a question like, "Is something wrong?" or "Are you upset about something?" You get a bonus point if you indicate you are considering what may be bothering her and say something like, "Was that a tough meeting?"

89. If she calls you and you can't talk, offer to call her back instead of having her call you back.

90. Return messages as promptly as possible. Calling back makes a big impression on Venus.

91. If she seems stressed or bothered, ask about it. You could say, "Is everything OK?" as an invitation for her to talk about it.

92. When you are frustrated or angry, avoid asking pointed questions. Take some time to cool off, and then ask her to help you understand the situation. By asking for her help she will not feel so attacked.

93. When dividing up responsibilities for doing a task together, give her a chance to express her wishes. You could say, "Let's work this out together. I would like to do this, but what do you think?" Or "I think this would be a good plan. How do you feel about it?"

94. When she has been away, let her know that her contribution is appreciated by telling her that she was missed. For example, "We missed you at the new site. Nobody knew what to do about . . ."

95. Celebrate the completion of little and big projects. Men and women greatly appreciate special occasions to celebrate or recognize people and their contributions. Give awards, certificates, or little presents.

96. Take a group picture including you and her at a conference and send her a copy.

97. Anticipate her needs and offer your assistance without her having to ask.

98. Repeat these small gestures of support as often as possible. Don't assume that once is enough.

99. Apologize or say excuse me when you make a mistake.

100. Confirm when you have done something.

101. If you have a wife and family, make sure you have pictures on them on your desk or on the wall. On the road have

them in your wallet so that you can share them. When a man appreciates his wife, other women also feel supported.

These tips present a checklist of ideas for men to summarize the many concepts found in *How To Get What You Want in the Workplace*. By remembering to do these little things, a wise man creates a supportive environment so that his big goals can be more effectively achieved.

Scoring Points on Mars

Men also appreciate little expressions of support, but often a man doesn't even notice a woman's support. For example, a man will certainly appreciate it if a woman asks him what he thinks, but if she doesn't, he may not even notice it and just say what he wanted to say. She makes a gesture of support, but it is not that important to him. On Mars the little things are nice but they are not as important as the big things.

If a man is stressed, he will not even notice the little things, but he will if he is relaxed. She may not get any points by focusing on little things. Ultimately, a woman scores most with men by doing the big things like making money, saving time, solving big problems, and coming up with productive ideas.

A woman scores most with men by doing the big things like making money.

On Mars, by focusing more on being productive and efficient, a woman will earn more points. If a little problem is solved, she scores fewer points. Ultimately on Mars, a woman is judged by the results she creates and how those results affect the bottom line. By creating results and then taking credit, she can earn the most points on Mars.

Although the bottom line scores the most points, even on Mars the little things can still make a big difference. When two people are competing for a promotion and both are equally qualified, what makes the difference is the extra little points that have been scored. Most sporting games are won by just a few points. The score in a basketball game generally seesaws to the end, and then one team wins by just a few points.

This is where women have a greater advantage in the workplace. Under stress, women tend to remember the little things, whereas men forget. If a woman learns how to score points with men, she can get ahead by remembering to score the little points. When all things are equal, it is the extra points that determine who gets ahead in the workplace.

To score extra points with men it is more complicated than just scoring points. Men give points, but also subtract points. This is common in competitive sports like football, baseball, and basketball. With one foul or mistake you can lose ten yards or possession of the ball. Without an understanding of how points are taken away, a woman can be very confused in the workplace and feel that it is very unfair.

To understand how to score points on Mars it is just as important to recognize how men take points away.

Equally important to understanding how to score points with men is recognizing why men take points away. For example, a woman may do a great job, but a man will subtract points if she complains about how difficult it was. He may give her lots of points for her efficiency, but then take them all away because she gets upset with something he says.

In the following list, to have a complete understanding of how to score points with men, "What not to do" is also emphasized. Keep in mind that some of the ways to score points with men may not be appropriate in all situations. Remember that when a man is under stress, he may not even notice your gestures of support, but he will notice your fouls. For this reason, an awareness of what not to do is very relevant on Mars.

As with any of the suggestions, keep in mind that one may work better for some men and may not be necessary with others. By reviewing this list you may get a glimpse of how you sabotage your success by giving the kind of support a woman would appreciate, but not what men want.

If misunderstood, this list can be discouraging to women. Many of the mistakes women make on Mars will cause them to lose five or ten points. It may seem as if women don't stand a chance or have to do everything right in order to get ahead. Remember that Martian penalties balance out a man's willingness to give a lot of points for getting the job done. For example, a woman gets a hundred points for suggesting a good idea or getting a project done in an efficient manner.

101 Ways for Women to Score Points with Men

1. Get to the point when making a suggestion. Avoid talking too much about problems. Remember, men hear sharing as complaining.
2. Only complain when you have a solution to suggest. Take less time to explain the problem and quickly move on to suggest a solution. The longer the time you take to complain, the more points you lose. The better your solution, the more points you will earn.
3. When conflict arises, be accepting of differences and don't take it personally. Taking offense or getting upset loses points. The more upset you get the more points you lose.
4. When a man forgets to do something, say something ac-

cepting like, "It's OK." An accepting attitude scores points. The bigger the mistake he makes, the more points you will get by being accepting and not punishing. You could get twenty points for overlooking a late delivery.

5. After asking for his advice, be careful not to correct his solution or explain in great detail why you are not going to follow his advice. By allowing him to save face, a woman can get lots of points. If his suggestion is confusing or weak, she gets even more points by not directly pointing that out.

6. Give advice only when it is welcome or solicited. Unsolicited advice causes her to lose points. Even if it is good advice she will still lose points.

7. Give credit and recognition whenever he has achieved something. If others have overlooked him or he really wants someone to notice, he will give you much more than one point. If he is feeling stressed, he may not notice it at all.

8. When taking credit, focus on what result you achieved instead of talking about how hard you worked. By talking about how much you sacrifice or how difficult something was, you may lose more points than you gained by achieving the result.

9. Be direct when you make a request. Don't talk about a problem and wait for him to offer his support. Often men feel manipulated when women are not direct. It is as if he "should do it" without her having to ask. The more he feels obligated to do something, the more he will take away points. She could easily lose five points.

10. When presenting a proposal or plan of action, talk less about the problem and more about what you think should be done. It is usually how much time you spend talking about the problem that determines how many points you will lose.

11. Be careful to minimize small talk around men. They will not appreciate mixing personal needs during work time. When men see women use work time to talk about personal issues they may take away points.

12. Be interested when men talk about sports. Take time to understand what they are talking about, but don't compete and appear to know more. Show your competence in areas that count to achieve the bottom line.

13. Compliment him when he has made a change to make himself look better. If he is in his cave and you interrupt what he is doing with a compliment, he may take a point away.

14. Show interest when he gets a new car or talks about cars. Be careful not to minimize his hobbies or other interests.

15. Dress in a way that makes you feel good about yourself and shows that you care about the way you look. Short skirts and tight sweaters are fine when it makes you feel good about you. Don't use your sex appeal to get points. If you are perceived as a tease, it may easily backfire and you will lose big points.

16. Wear less makeup. Most men don't like it and will take away a point. If you wear makeup to feel confident, then wear it because the points you gain by being confident will easily cancel out the one point you lose.

17. When he makes a moan or groan, give him more space rather than a sympathetic pat on the back. Avoid doing anything that demonstrates a feeling of motherly empathy. Giving sympathy is a turn off, and he will take away points. If he is really upset, he will take away more points.

18. Be optimistic about his success. Unless he directly asks for your help, don't express your worries and concerns. In a cheerful manner, wish him luck and you may earn five points.

19. Acknowledge the things he has done for you with a tone of

appreciation. Don't make a big deal out of it, but don't overlook it either.

20. When a man offers to help, let him help and then appreciate his assistance. Whenever a man succeeds in helping a woman and feels appreciated, he will feel more connected to her.

21. Minimize his mistakes. When he makes a mistake and you don't make a big deal out of it, a man feels extra support. The bigger the mistake that she minimizes, the more points she will get.

22. In public build him up. If you want to point out a mistake or suggest a change, do it in private. Depending on who hears this correction, he will feel more embarrassed and you will lose more points.

23. When you get up to get a drink of water, offer to get him a glass as well.

24. When he is in a hurry, don't bring up personal problems. This may not earn points, but it will sure keep you from losing a lot.

25. Be accepting and relaxed when he is in his cave. Don't ask if everything is OK. Untimely interruptions lose points.

26. In a group meeting, graciously interrupt. Don't say, "Can I say something?" Instead, go with the flow and say something more friendly like, "That's true, I think . . ."

27. Use a relaxed and trusting tone of voice when discussing work problems. Men are repelled by the tone of being emotionally overwhelmed. The more overwhelmed a woman is the more points a man will take away.

28. Stay focused on the task at hand and postpone the need to share personal feelings. Keep your work life and personal life separate.

29. When you ask questions, make sure they are not rhetorical or backed by negative emotions. Rhetorical questions backed by negative emotions lose ten to twenty points.

30. When asking for support, keep your emotions out of it and focus on stating what you want. Take time to justify your request if you are asked why you need more.

31. Say no graciously. A man is turned off when a woman tells him how much she has to do as a way of saying no. From his perspective, a simple "I can't do it" is enough. If he wants to know more, he will ask. The more you justify your need to say no by sharing your difficulties and problems, the more points you lose with him.

32. She gets a point by not taking offense at Martian jokes that aren't funny to her. If a joke doesn't fly, she gets points by not ridiculing it or showing disgust. Putting down his jokes loses points.

33. When complaining to your manager or coworker, be objective and avoid making value judgments like, "It's not fair" or "He isn't doing his job." Instead say, "He was three hours late. I was the only one there to do a job that requires two people." The more calm and objective you are the more points your argument gets. You may have a worthy complaint, but if you get emotional it will seem less worthy.

34. If there is too much being expected of you, ask for the support you need, but don't complain. Men take away points when someone complains about overworking. He reasons, "Don't waste time complaining, instead do something to get the support you need."

35. When a man gives you his card, take time to look at it and read it with a little nod of recognition.

36. When a man has pictures or awards on his walls, ask about them or notice them with an interested or impressed tone of voice.

37. In a discussion, make supportive comments like "That makes sense" or "Good idea" from time to time.

38. When he is making a presentation or discussing something, don't be overly eager or automatically reassuring while listening. Let him feel that he is earning your agreement and support. Too much eagerness loses points.

39. When disappointed, be forgiving. Give men opportunities to prove themselves. On Mars, you get three strikes before you are out. Even then you get eight more innings to make a comeback if you are behind. The bigger his mistake, the more points you earn by forgiving him.

40. Pace yourself. After listening to a man, let him know that something is helpful before you bring up more issues or questions. In conversation, when a man makes a point and you do not acknowledge it, he will penalize you a point. By continuing to acknowledge the points a man makes, you can score ten points while listening to him.

41. When a man doesn't follow your advice and then makes a mistake, you can score a point by holding back from the temptation to say, "I told you so." By not saying anything, he is even more aware of the advice you gave and appreciative that you are not putting it in his face. The bigger his mistake, the more points you get. On the other hand, by saying, "I told you so," she may lose five points.

42. When a man disappoints you, be friendly and accepting by making statements like, "It's not a problem" or "No big deal, you can just do it tomorrow."

43. Make sure he hears or overhears you talking about him or other men in a positive light.

44. Share your experience to back up a request and don't quote an expert. For example, don't say, "John Gray says you should listen to me more. . . ." Instead say, "I would appreciate it if you would listen a little longer before responding."

45. Don't quote "experts" to tell a man what he should do or how he could improve unless he is directly asking.

46. Don't ask questions about the status of your working relationship. For example, don't say, "Do you think I am doing a good job?" Instead you could say, "Did you like this report?" By making your request for reassurance less personal you don't lose a point.

47. Let a man know up front how much time you expect a meeting to last. You get extra points for staying to the point and on schedule.

48. As a manager, limit giving directions to the absolute minimum. The more independence he gets, the more he will appreciate you.

49. As a manager, depersonalize your directions with comments like, "We are expected to . . ." or "I have been told we need to . . ." and then ask him to do what you want with a request phrase like, "Would you . . ." or "Please . . ."

50. Be careful not to sound condescending by "scolding" a man. For example, don't say, "You are not listening to me." Instead say, "Let me try saying this differently."

51. Give a personal greeting and use his name when arriving in the workplace. Then ask a friendly business question.

52. Acknowledge him by regarding something he did or accomplished in the workplace. For example, "I saw the report you wrote. It was really great."

53. Take time to acknowledge in front of others some recent success or accomplishment of his.

54. When a man comes in the room and you are sitting, stand up and shake hands as equals.

55. Take interest in his personal life by asking questions during casual breaks, not during work time.

56. Overlook his deficiencies and have an accepting attitude about his imperfection. For example, avoid noticing and pointing out his fatigue or stress level. Don't say in a sympathetic tone, "You look tired" or "What's wrong?"

57. When stress increases, act as if everything is OK. Worrying or showing concern about him can be offensive. A more relaxed response demonstrates a level of trust that says, "I'm sure you can handle it."

58. If he makes an unwanted sexual advance or comment, nip it in the bud by making a clear statement that you are not interested without showing disapproval or offense. The more offended you are the more points you will lose.

59. Know his favorite sports teams. If they do well, congratulate him. Even though he didn't win he feels as if he did. The more important the victory the more points you can get.

60. Notice if he gets a new car, and ask to go for a drive with others. At least look at it and let him talk about it. Show him the same degree of interest you would demonstrate when a girlfriend talks about her new wedding gown. This could earn ten points. Men like to show off things in the same way that women like to share secrets.

61. If you are in a supportive role, rather than do everything in an invisible manner, sometimes ask in a friendly tone, "Would you like me to . . ." In this way, he realizes how much you do and can give you the points you deserve.

62. Make sure that you take credit for your achievements and that you don't attribute them to good luck or to someone else. You get a point for taking credit and then many more for what you did. For a little project it may be fifty points and for a bigger success it could be a hundred points. By not taking credit when it is done you will not be penalized, but you will not earn the hundred points you deserve.

63. When things get difficult, don't complain. You get a point for hanging in there and "being a good trooper."

64. When he is on a business trip, have the hotel welcome him with a message and include information like times for

sporting events, a business magazine, newspaper, the location of a gym or a TV guide.

65. Remember his birthday and send a card, take him to lunch,
or have an office party so everyone can sing "Happy Birthday" with a dessert.

66. On business trips or journeys, offer to drive, and don't assume that he will because he is a man. If he drives, make
sure to appreciate him at the end. If he drives, let him drive
and avoid backseat driving instructions.

67. If he seems lost, avoid suggesting that he should get directions. He may take it personally as a sign that you don't
trust him to get where he wants to go.

68. If he gets lost, make the best of it and don't complain or tell
others. The more lost he was, the more points she will get.

69. When you get angry, stop talking, take a few deep
breaths, and drink a glass of water. By clearly holding
back your anger, he will respect you more. To him it will
demonstrate that you are being accountable and not making him responsible for how you feel. When he doesn't
feel blamed, he is actually more willing to hear what you
want to say.

70. Don't ask a man how he feels about something; instead ask
what he thinks about something. By appreciating his logic,
you can score a point.

71. Whenever possible, let a man know when he was right.
When you point out his correctness, he gives you a point.

72. When conveying a message, don't keep adding things to it.
Avoid saying, "Hmm, what else did I want to tell you?" or
"Oh, one more thing." Being concise scores points and
wandering around will lose points.

73. If you leave written messages, number your points and
write clearly.

74. In a business setting in which many people are being intro-

duced, introduce yourself so that the male host doesn't have to remember everyone's name and introduce each person.

75. When introducing a man to others, always include his accomplishments, expertise, or role in the company.

76. Practice saying what you do so that in one minute you can clearly explain what you do in a way that includes your expertise and talents. By introducing yourself and letting others know your expertise, you immediately get a point.

77. When making small talk during breaks, make sure that he is interested and that he is not just being polite by listening.

78. When making small talk, if you do most of the talking, you can score a point by saying, "It was really nice talking with you."

79. In a group meeting, take time to point out or to acknowledge the value of his contribution before making your own points.

80. In a group meeting, when you disagree or are challenged by others, stick to your argument and do not digress by sharing how you personally feel. The more offended or upset you get, the more points you will lose. You may have a better argument, but will not get credit because of your delivery.

81. If he has pictures of family members on his desk, ask about them and share briefly about your family.

82. On a business trip, if he mentions his family, ask if he brought any pictures and show interest if he pulls them out of his wallet. When a man is proud of his family, you will definitely get extra points.

83. If he sneezes, say, "Bless you." You may, however, lose points if you proceed to ask more questions about his cold and then offer advice.

84. If he spills something, get up and get a towel to help clean up the mess. Unless it is your job requirement, don't do it

all. Make sure he helps clean up his mess as well. If you say, "I'll handle it," he may easily overlook your assistance as a job requirement. Instead say, "Let me help."

85. If he has a cold, offer him some Kleenex but don't make any suggestions to improve him. For example, don't say, "If you didn't work so hard you wouldn't have gotten sick."

86. When an argument becomes emotionally charged, grace-fully take a break. Say something like, "Give me some time to think about this and then let's talk again." Overcome the temptation to say, "You're not being fair" or "You are not listening to me."

87. When telling stories with a lot of characters involved, men-tion the names again and again. A man will sometimes for-get who they, he, or she is.

88. When a man makes a suggestion or gives a solution that you were already planning to do, make it clear in a face-saving manner that you had already come up with the same solution. Otherwise, you will get no points and he will give himself points. If the solution was obvious, and he con-cluded that you needed his help, you will lose points.

89. When a man is grumpy, ignore it and act as if everything is fine. By not drawing attention to his bad mood, he will be very appreciative later. The more grumpy he was, the more points you will get for ignoring him.

90. When he only has to ask once for something to get done, you will get more points. On Mars and Venus, they take away points for having to ask more than once. The differ-ence on Mars is that if you forget to do something small but do something big, you don't lose a point.

91. If a woman has lost points by getting emotional about something, she can gain them back plus more by briefly apologizing or saying, "Excuse me for that outburst." If

she dwells too long on the apology or gives a lot of details to explain it, she will lose even more points.

92. Recognize that most men don't like being told what to do. Don't take it personally. If your job requires that you give him instructions, to minimize the inevitable tension, prepare him by saying, "Is this a good time to review some changes?" or "Let's schedule a time when we can meet. I have some changes I need to convey."

93. When dividing up tasks, be clear about what you want. You get points for clarity if you know what you want and then even more points if you make a reasonable compromise. Women don't get points for seeming uncertain and going along with what he decides.

94. Appreciate a man's way of dividing up responsibilities and you will get a point.

95. When you haven't seen him for a while, let him know that his contribution is appreciated by telling him that he was missed. For example, "We missed you last week. Nobody knew what to do about . . ." Make sure that it doesn't sound like a complaint that he wasn't there.

96. Celebrate the completion of a long or important project. Men and women greatly appreciate special occasions to celebrate or recognize people and their contributions. Give awards, certificates, or little presents. When big rewards are given, men give more points.

97. When a man does something, offer to take a picture of him with the finished product. The bigger the fish he catches, the more he will appreciate someone taking the picture.

98. On the phone, when you don't have the answer to a question, rather than taking his time trying to remember, simply say, "I don't have that information, I'll get right back to you."

99. Score more points by being personally supportive when he is out of his cave.

100. Don't quickly let on if you don't have an answer or a solution. Always appear confident. Avoid the phrase "I don't know." Instead say something like, "I am still working that one out."

101. Take credit for your achievements by displaying awards, certificates, and degrees on the walls of your office. Display pictures of you with successful people or involved with different work projects. If he shows interest, describe your success with a tone of confidence.

This list heps to summarize for women the many concepts found in *How To Get What You Want in the Workplace*. By reviewing this list at times when she feels confused by working with men, a woman can begin to make sense of what happened. A wise woman is careful of the many ways she can lose points with men to insure that she gets the full credit she deserves for her accomplishments.

13

Remembering Our Differences

Next time you are frustrated or resentful about someone of the opposite sex, take some time to reflect on what you have read in *How To Get What You Want in the Workplace*. Just pick up the book and read a few pages. Your perspective will expand. By remembering once again how men and women are different and that we are supposed to be that way, we are set free from unnecessary judgments and instead experience increasing understanding, acceptance, and respect. By taking responsibility to change yourself instead of waiting for others to change, you will feel and exercise your new power to create positive and supportive work relationships.

After studying and applying this guide for improving communication and getting results at work you will begin to get more of what you want. Just recognizing our differences can bring us more clarity in understanding why people react the way they do. Automatically, confusing or frustrating interactions begin to make more sense. You are able to be more accepting of others as well as yourself.

On another level, with this insight, you are empowered to make better choices in how you respond to others. By recognizing what planet a man or woman is coming from, you are able to behave in a more appropriate manner that earns you the respect and trust you deserve.

Finally, at a third level, the workplace becomes a better place for all. By serving as an example of someone who can bridge our different worlds, you are leading the way for others to do the same. As more men and women come together in greater harmony and appreciation, the workplace can begin to reflect our highest aspirations for humanity.

A better work life is not enough. These inspiring results cannot fully be achieved unless your work life is supported by a fulfilling home life as well. For most, it is unrealistic to expect the workplace to be your only source of fulfillment. Finding the right balance for you between work and home is essential for a personally fulfilling and successful life.

With a commitment to achieving this balance and a new understanding of how to earn the respect and trust of the opposite sex, you are well prepared. You have good reason to feel hopeful. By returning again and again to review the differences between men and women in the workplace, you will be able to revive this newfound feeling of confidence and inspiration.

I have witnessed thousands of men and women who have experienced immediate success by using these important insights. Within a few days of attending a Mars-Venus workshop, men and women find that communication improves and cooperation increases in their work relationships. With this support they start getting what they want. Challenges that were difficult in the past suddenly become easier. By applying the insights you have gained through reading this book and by remembering that men are from Mars and women are from Venus you will experience the same success.

The process of learning anything new takes time. Reading

and applying these ideas once is not enough. To develop a truly new thinking pattern or behavior, it takes forgetting and then remembering many times. Although the many ideas of *How To Get What You Want in the Workplace* make sense, they are deceptively simple and not as easy to remember and put in action. When you review them you realize how much you have forgotten.

When we are under stress, we often react, think, and respond from our instincts and habits. Men instinctively behave in a way that is appreciated most on Mars, and women as on Venus. To earn the respect and trust of the opposite sex in the workplace, we have to respond in ways that are counterinstinctive. Fortunately, this can be learned, but it does take practice.

Applying these new insights is like learning to ski. When skiing down a slope, you have to lean forward or else you cannot turn. Leaning forward on a steep slope is counterinstinctive. When faced with this challenge your body pulls back. This reaction is overcome by practice, and eventually leaning forward becomes automatic. Although it is not "natural," it becomes a skier's natural stance.

To succeed at work, men and women need to put on different hats at different times. Sometimes we are required to respond in a way that the opposite sex understands and sometimes we can relax and behave in a manner that is accepted on our own planet. This shifting back and forth requires increased flexibility and stability. As you practice applying these new insights, you too will be able to shift back and forth connecting our different worlds. This shift will become as graceful and automatic as skiing down a hill.

There has never been a greater time for positive change to occur. As men and women come closer together in the workplace to meet this challenge, we are required to reach within ourselves and find a new way of interacting. By stretching ourselves so that both men and women get more of the respect and support they deserve, the workplace can and will become a better place for ourselves and for generations to come.

Share this book with your friends, managers, and coworkers but in a way that doesn't say they really need it. When a woman presents this book to a man, she needs to do it respectfully. Telling him he really needs it may sound like criticism and be a turn-off. Instead, ask him to underline any of the issues that he thinks are important for women to understand about men.

Give him the book so that he can tell you if the ideas about men are really true. Just have him look over the list of 101 ways a woman can score points with men and ask him which of the points are true for him. Instead of pointing out how he needs this book, which is inappropriate even if he does, ask him to help you understand men better. Men love to be experts. After being exposed to these insights, if it is for him he will read on.

You have a lot to look forward to. Thank you for letting me make a difference in your life. May you have a more fulfilling work experience and continue to experience greater success. May this book be a little candle to guide your way through the darkness of confusion and prejudice into the light of clarity and compassion. Thank you for your efforts. Every step you take brings us all closer to creating a world of peace, equality and justice for all.

Vermilion books are available from all good
bookshops or call our mail order hotline
number on:
01206 255 800

Postage and packing is free

For a Mars and Venus counsellor/trainer in the
UK contact: Ina Sanderson PhD
Mars Venus (UK) Ltd
PO Box 6158
Northants
NN18 8ZB
tel +44 (0) 1536 743 997
fax +44 (0) 1536 460 441
email: mvdirect@mars-venus.co.uk
www.mars-venus.co.uk